MW00579120

WHAT TO DO WHEN LIFE
WHEN LIFE
sucks

WHAT TO DO WHEN LIFE SUCKS

PROVEN STRATEGIES FOR
EMOTIONAL TRAUMA PREVENTION,
INTERVENTION, AND
POST-TRAUMATIC GROWTH

FRAN GRAHAM

International Emergency Management
and Emotional Trauma Specialist

WHAT TO DO WHEN LIFE SUCKS
© 2021 Fran Graham.

All rights reserved. No part of this publication may be reproduced, distributed, or transmitted in any form or by any means, including photocopying, recording, or other electronic or mechanical methods, without the prior written permission of the publisher, except in the case of brief quotations embodied in critical reviews and certain other noncommercial uses permitted by copyright law. For permission requests, please contact the author.

Published by Fran Graham | Victor, Montana

ISBN (Print): 978-1-7366023-0-0

ISBN (Kindle): 978-1-7366023-1-7

Printed in the United States of America

Prepared for Publication: www.wendykwalters.com

Unless otherwise indicated, all Scripture quotations are taken from the Amplified® Bible (AMPC), Copyright © 1954, 1958, 1962, 1964, 1965, 1987 by The Lockman Foundation. Used by permission. www.lockman.org.

To contact the author: WWW.FRANHGRAHAM.COM

DEDICATION

Without the experience of terrible pain, trauma, loss, grief, and many of life's difficulties, both for me and the many people I've had the humble privilege to help, this book wouldn't exist. Those stressful and often tragic situations taught me what I know now, and as awful as they were, they created the material for this book, therefore, I'm thankful for them. So, this book is dedicated to three groups of people. Those I've helped along the way; people who've risen again and are experiencing post-traumatic growth. Well done! I'm so proud of you for not allowing yourselves to stay where you once were.

It's dedicated to my chaplain comrades, first responders, doctors, dispatchers, pastors, therapists, and anyone else who tirelessly goes above and beyond, again and again, to care for those in need. Hopefully, this will encourage you to take more time for yourself so that you're able to keep doing what you do for the long haul.

Lastly, it's also dedicated to you, the reader, because I wrote it for you so that you, too, can learn to breathe again when life sucks, and you've had the wind knocked out of you. Rise Again to new life and pay it forward.

Resurgam!

WHAT TO DO WHEN LIFE SUCKS

ACKNOWLEDGMENTS

There are so many incredible people who've helped me become who I am today. Too many to mention here. So instead, I'll mention those who've been there to pick me up, dust me off, show me how to breathe in that life-giving air when I've had the wind knocked out of me, and point me in the right direction so that I can rise again, learn from each experience and pay it forward. Without all of them, this book wouldn't exist, because I wouldn't have learned what I now know, so I wouldn't have written it!

To Rob, my amazing husband and best friend. You've never questioned my craziness and you allow me to follow my dreams and passions, no matter where they take me, even with or without you. You've always been right by my side. You're faithful, loyal, loving and kind. Over the years you've learned to monitor the warning signs that I've overdone things. If I miss them, which even now I sometimes do, or if I push myself too far, you speak up. When that happens, I know I need to stop what I'm doing, take a break and reassess my self-care. You're my most important sounding board, supporting me no matter what and encouraging me to follow my calling as I disappear again and again, into the unknown worlds of trauma, national and international deployments and speaking engagements, local chaplain calls in the middle of the night, and everything in between. You've been patient when the calls or deployments have come at inconvenient times and interrupted our family life. You've never complained, not even once! You're there for me when I come home exhausted, often heartbroken and in need of TLC and a listening ear. You always work so hard to make ends meet, and have happily covered the costs of my work, when possible. Thank you for your selfless love and constant encouragement. You are my hero, Rob. I love you deeply, to eternity, and I'm so abundantly blessed that you're mine!

To my four amazing sons, three daughters-in-law and two grandchildren. Robbie, Helen, Lucas, Isabel, Nick, James, Meghan, Alex and Leeanna. You are my soul-food and the lights of my life. You, together with Dad/Papa, are my favorite people to be with. You are the first people I run to, and need to be with, when I return home from deployments or difficult chaplaincy calls. Thank you for speaking truth into my life when I need it. Thank you all for putting up with my intense need of, and love for, our family, which has deepened more and more with each deployment, because of the realization that there by the grace of God we go, and that one day, one of us may not be here. Thank you all for the constant laughter, which always restores my soul. Thank you for being my cheer leaders and a special thank you to Lucas and Isabel for the best snuggles ever!

Thanks to my favorite cop, baker, European ally, and sourdough teacher, Keld Hove. Words can't express the impact you've had in my life in so many ways. Without my sourdough bread baking, I wouldn't have been able to manage many of the painful experiences I've had. Your friendship, playful banter and challenging sourdough quizzes have given me different perspectives, brought me joy, and have made me view life in different ways. Baking has helped to restore my soul by giving me a positive outlet. One that I can share with others when I give them a fresh loaf, or when I share the baking knowledge with them that you continue to share with me. Together we pay it forward.

To Robby Booth, who recognized my gifts and unique calling many years ago. You're the one who told me that I'd make a good chaplain and the rest is history! You showed me the way and guided me into chaplaincy. Thank you, Robby, for the many hours you've dedicated to me as a dear friend, therapist, prayer partner and encourager. Especially when I've crashed and burned and needed someone to process my deepest pain and struggles with, that were too deep to manage on my own or by just talking to Rob. I wouldn't be where I am today, doing what I love most, without you, your counsel, love and support.

To Naomi Paget, my friend, mentor, advisor, encourager, and the best Critical Incident Stress Management teacher in the world. Naomi, you taught me most of what I know about managing stress and trauma, and how to help others through their pain. Thank you, my friend, for your excellent courses and for being so faithful to always show me the way forward in my work. And I can't leave out the crucial fact that you certainly know how to show me a good time and expand my self-care activities by being my cruising bunkmate and precious gem buying-buddy. Ha-ha. As I've mentioned to you before, I want to be just like you when I grow up ;)

To Felisa Hamman and Susan Gaddis, my self-care partners in crime. You've both been by my side through thick and thin. You make me laugh, get me into mischief, soak in hot tubs with me, travel to fun and relaxing places, play games and pranks, and comfort me when I cry. You lovingly cared for me through my cancer journey when Rob wasn't available. You prayed for me, helped me to put one foot in front of the other and take each step towards healing one day at a time. Thank you Felisa and Susan for keeping the laughter going, for teaching me how to pull up my big girl panties, and for challenging me when I need it most. I love you both dearly and am so thankful for you.

And finally, to Wendy Walters, my amazing editor, friend and the one and only person who was able to pull this book out of me. You made me believe that I could do this. You made me declare that I was an author and a finisher, and you gave me a special pen to sign my books with when people want a signed copy. I have it ready and waiting to be used! Your incredible love, patience, friendship, encouragement and dedication made this book a reality. You even knew when to kick my rear when I needed it and refocus me when I was going in the wrong direction, both with my writing discipline and my story line. Oh, and my jacket cover! You're such a trooper! Your excellence and very high standards in your work, together with many hours of editing, branding, re-editing, designing, challenging me, believing in me, publishing advice, and everything else in between has made my dream a reality. This book would never have happened without you. I am now an author, and I did finish! Thank you, Wendy, from the bottom of my heart.

PRAISE FOR WHAT TO DO WHEN LIFE SUCKS

Chaplain Fran is a special gift to the body of Christ. Her expertise in responding to trauma brings what many view as a transactional relationship into a transformational deposit from her heart into the healing and the emotional well-being of those she serves. Fran takes the most detailed information about how our brains process trauma and stress and synthesizes that data into a holistic platform. *What To Do When Life Sucks*, as an academic exercise, is guaranteed to make a lasting impression on your emotional walk and your ability to foresee problematic situations beginning to arise in your life so that you will be well-equipped to handle these matters in a healthy manner.

Dr. John Wheeler III
Executive Vice President
Faith International University

In this era of such suffering in our world, Fran has written an important practitioner's guide to understanding and experiencing holistic health. As an esteemed chaplain who has been a first responder in many critical incidents as well as walking her own path toward healing, she has witnessed the power of friends on the journey coupled with the attending grace and love of Jesus Christ. This book is a must-read for those in helping professions and those of us in need of help.

Tammy Dunahoo
Vice President of U.S. Operations
The Foursquare Church

One of the greatest gifts to anyone suffering from acute and critical incident stress is someone who has already walked the journey. Fran Graham's book *What To Do When Life Sucks* is exactly that kind of gift. Courageously transparent and faithful to the ministry of healing, offering insights and truths that inspire readers to rise above the life-altering effects of exposure to stress, grief, and trauma. First responders, chaplains, and disaster relief workers will find this book a valuable resource for themselves and those they serve.

Chaplain Jason Reynolds,
Director of Foursquare Chaplains International & Foursquare Disaster Relief-US
Lead Chaplain, Harvey County Sheriff's Office/Newton Police Department,
Newton, KS

Early in my career, I responded to a report of a structure fire with injuries. I was deeply affected by the impact of treating and caring for a three-year-old girl who suffered extensive second-degree burns. The memory of looking into her silent crying eyes is something I will never forget. If it had not been for the empathy and guidance of someone like Pastor Fran Graham, someone skilled in understanding Critical Incident Stress Management, I would never have been able to continue in my chosen profession. *What To Do When Life Sucks* is a story of singular courage amongst hardship, defined by her experience and wisdom, and clearly identifies the steps necessary to aid in the healing process. Fran has seamlessly woven her personal story into the framework necessary to battle the impacts of traumatic events. Her passion is clear; she wants you to rise again.

William S. Hollingworth, Fire Chief
San Luis Obispo County Critical Incident Stress Management Coordinator, CA.

Fran doesn't pull any punches, not with her insistence that everyone should understand how to prepare for and handle stress and trauma, nor with the re-telling of her own life-changing experiences. This makes for a powerful blend of practical and personal insight and results in a book that is as relevant to frontline responders as it is to anyone who might be unexpectedly thrust into dealing with a traumatic incident.

Anonymous
For Security Reasons

What To Do When Life Sucks was an easy-to-read soulful conversation with a wise friend. Fran uses a healthy blend of research, science, faith, and her own legitimate personal and professional trauma experiences to illustrate the path to living, not just existing. As a 30+ year fire service veteran, the book had a surprising sweetness and refreshing tone on tough topics. This book will validate and empower responders and their families.

Laurie Donnelly
Battalion Chief (retired)

As human beings, there are survival skills that we all need to maintain our mental, emotional, and spiritual health. Fran Graham takes readers on a journey through her life experiences and reveals how to use these vital life skills to face traumatic life events with the confidence and strength to not only survive but to rise again and thrive.

Ben Harris
Executive Director of Tacoma-Pierce County Chaplaincy

What To Do When Life Sucks is an appropriate sharing of Fran's life. She shares examples that make sense and help with understanding. Fran is sound, and her input is needful and from a strong Scripture base.

It is insightful! Fran helps people understand themselves as well as understand people who have gone through difficult issues. As a result of Fran's insights, caring people can receive the tools to benefit those who are hurting by offering help.

In a world that seems to have an ever-growing amount of difficulty, this book becomes a must-have for people who desire to help others in pain. It can make the difference between furthering their pain and easing their pain.

Fran comes with her own giftedness and a deep well of understanding trauma and experience in ministering to people in trauma. The principles she outlines in this book work for individuals as well as groups and crosses all geographical, age, gender, and ethnic boundaries.

It's powerful and empowering for those that desire to help and a welcome read for all those in helping professions so they can be helpful for the long-haul and not burn out or suffer other fallouts.

Robby Booth, MA (MFCC).
Director of the Center for Spiritual Renewal West.

CONTENTS

YOU MAY HAVE TO FIGHT A
BATTLE MORE THAN ONCE
TO WIN IT.

MARGARET THATCHER

SOMETIMES LIFE SUCKS

WHAM! What the...? Knocked down to the ground without warning. Can't breathe. Dazed and confused. Still can't breathe. Chest hurts. Stomach feels as if you've been punched. Panic and fear set in as you try to make your lungs work. Nope, still can't get any air, even though you try to suck it back into your lungs. Frustration and desperation set in as you try again and again. Finally, after what seems like a long time, you manage to inhale a small amount at first. Then after a while, as your diaphragm relaxes, your breaths become deeper, the fear of suffocation dissipates, causing you to relax too. No, you're not going to suffocate. You are not going to die. Not today anyway. But when you're knocked or thrown down so hard that you're winded and all breath escapes you, it can be frightening. When you can't breathe, you panic. Thoughts of death bombard you.

And so it is with emotional trauma. It crashes into your life, throwing you to the ground, usually without any warning. In that moment, your life sucks, and that fact sucks any remaining life out of you, or so it seems. It crushes you. Suffocating you, causing you to feel smothered and unable to breathe under the emotional weight of what's just happened. With every gasp of air you try to suck back into your lungs, you are literally fighting for your life because you know that without air, you will die. This is what emotional trauma, grief, shock, and acute stress can feel like. And yet, you can still breathe, albeit in small amounts. As your survival instinct kicks in, it forces you to suck more and more air back into your lungs again. You slowly recover and rise to your feet again. When life's knocks and hardships suck the life and breath out of you, your only way to survive is to suck air back into your lungs as hard as you can. How?

Enter the forest.

Forests call to me—lush, green, moist, and freshly filled with a hushed silence in the air. My sanctuary is always found in a forest, away from the crowds, and preferably by a babbling brook or flowing stream that leads to a waterfall where the crashing power of the water sprays me with fresh, ice-cold drops of precipitation that awaken my dulled senses. I come alive in the forest. The deeper I go into my private green world amongst these magnificent trees, the more my senses are quickened as I ponder the wonder of nature, of creation, of life itself. The noisy business of the world fades away, and I'm left with myself, with my senses, and with the abundance of raw, natural, untouched forest life surrounding me. The silence is loud, drowning out all chaos. I can hear only my breath and the twigs crackling under my feet as I tread softly on the forest debris covering the path. The forest is my safe place, and I only invite very special friends to come here with me from time to time, but usually, I prefer to go alone. In the forest is where I feel revived, recharged, and where I give myself space to ponder the challenges of life that confront me. This is where I come to be quiet—attend my thoughts, heed my heart, and listen to God.

As I make time to take it all in and look around, I see the various phases of life everywhere; the colors, the smells, the sights of old life, new life, and tall trees that cover the hillside on my left and my right. Today there is no wind. It's just quiet. Occasionally, the warm sun breaks through the trees and falls on my face, warming my skin, lighting the path as I explore. It invites me to go deeper, to trust it with my inner thoughts, fears, questions, and answers about life itself. I usually find answers in ways that surprise me. Ferns grow around dead tree stumps, and little beetles and insects scurry about in piles of decaying wood without paying any attention to me. As I wander further through the forest, I notice the death, decay, and destruction of many trees that have fallen naturally or have been felled; left to lie in place so that their rotting wood is naturally recycled to feed the ground which once fed its roots giving it nutrition to sustain life.

I don't know when or why my deep love for forests began, but my earliest recollection of feeling like this was when I was a small child. I've just always loved the atmosphere and scenery of forests, and when I'm there, I feel so incredibly close to nature, to my true self, to God. It's just me and Him and His amazing creation. I can be raw, honest, and real about my joys, my woes, my fears, and my successes there. I can be silent, or I can sing. I can cry, or I can laugh, and the forest just lovingly covers me with its boughs, as if protecting me, allowing me just to be free to be who I am and to express whatever

3

needs to flow out of my heart. The forest is always brutally honest with me. It never lies to me, never hides its miraculous stories of new birth and thriving species or its tragic stories of death. It just lays it out there for all to see.

Through nature, God always teaches me so much about the cycle of life as I pay attention to its examples. Every living thing goes through struggles to survive, and yes, sometimes even to thrive in this cruel but marvelous world. I look for signs of new life. It's all around. New fresh flowers in the spring. New shoots of baby trees poking up through the ground. Baby ferns tightly curled, waiting to mature and unfurl their majestic leaves. But there's an even more miraculous sign of life for which I look. I look for the life that comes from a tragic death, the life that comes from apparent destruction. Then I see it. There's always that special one that catches my eye. Oh, what a story it holds, if only it could talk. But there it is, a broken, damaged tree stump that appears to be slowly decaying, its life fading away into the ground that once fed it and held it up tall and strong.

I search all over the debris and in the nooks and crannies of the seemingly dead stump for that one clue, the one miracle that always makes me wonder and marvel at the phenomenal power of creation. There it is! I see it. A tiny new green shoot of life is emerging from the dead-looking stump. A beautiful sign that proves that no matter what the tree looks like on the outside, no matter how dead and damaged it looks, no matter what nature or man has done to it, it is still able to survive the harshest of weathers, storms, fires, accidents, and even man-made destruction. As long as its roots are left in the ground, no matter how dead the stump looks, new life can always rise again. ***Resurgam!***

This is what I call a *Resurgam moment.* The word Resurgam is Latin, meaning "I shall rise again." Resurgam has been our family's motto on my father's side for hundreds of years, and over the centuries, my ancestors certainly had to stand on that declaration. They've been attacked, injured, lost everything, experienced tragedies, fought in wars, faced betrayal, died of diseases, and have had their hearts broken. Despite all of that, the family survived. It lives on today in me and my children, and we're still standing. After many blows, we still rise again and carry on, without surrender, without turning back, and without believing that all is lost.

RESURGAM *(Latin).*

"I SHALL RISE AGAIN."

Our family stands on our faith that we can, and will, all rise again—and we have done so, generation after generation. But gone are the days when that motto meant our family would return to societal greatness, to wealth, or a place of honor in the Scottish clans. What does Resurgam mean to us today, or more specifically, to you? Well, every family and every person goes through some of those painful seasons mentioned above. My family certainly isn't unique in that area. But what makes us rise again is that we never give up. We get back on our feet time and time again and keep moving forward. We keep rising again and again—as many times as we need to so that we can finish well.

Imagine that you're a tree. If you are one tree standing alone, you're never as protected as you are if you're surrounded by a few other trees. In a forest, you are the most protected. As it is with trees, so it is with humans. In solitude, we have less protection than when we are in a group, and as we grow together in meaningful relationships, that network of people becomes our forest of protection. In our forest, some of us are thriving, and others aren't doing so well. Some are just starting out in life, and others' lives are ending, but the circle of life never ends. The compost from one rotting tree nourishes the next tree, giving it new life. We continuously give life to one another in some way. We rely on each other for our survival. With that idea in mind, I'd love to invite you on a journey with me as I share my family's declaration with you. As we explore the concept of becoming a new forest of stronger trees, I'll show you how you can have Resurgam moments and how you, too, can rise again from the depths of trauma and tragedy.

⋖〜☙☙☙☙〜⋗

Acute stress causes ill health. To be restored to full health requires significant change. This book will talk about emotional death and survival, mental death and healing, behavioral death and change, spiritual death, and new life. Whether or not your belief system includes God, my conviction is that He loves you deeply, cares about your needs, and has answers for you in times of turmoil.

Jesus, the great teacher, is the very picture of Resurgam. Life sucked for Him in so many ways, just as it does for you and me. But all along, He kept breathing in the goodness, healing power, and wisdom of God, even to the point of death and beyond. After dying on the cross, He descended into hell—breathless, with all life extinguished—and was there for three days. But in His Resurgam moment, He breathed, filling His lungs with life-giving air, then rose again, resembling new life and a new beginning!

As you read, you'll notice that I present two different perspectives. One from a personal point of view, sharing my journey through various traumatic events. The other perspective is that of a first responder and caregiver to those in distress. I'll switch back and forth to show both sides in the hopes that it will give you a more rounded understanding of what to do when life sucks, whether it's your life or someone else's. However, this book wasn't written like a psychological journal, covering all aspects of mental and emotional disorders. It's written in plain English, and is a basic, introduction to the very broad subject of trauma; a foundation, so to speak, for further education and training.

Are you ready to take that deep, life-giving breath? Come walk among the trees with me. Find your footing in the forest of strong survivors. Let's visit together and work through the trauma and tragedies you have borne until new shoots of life begin to sprout from the places in your soul you thought were dormant or perhaps even dead. This book will guide you through a proven process of healing and recovery.

Most importantly, it will lead you into a period of post-traumatic growth—a unique kind of personal transformation made possible only as you emerge from life's hard places. It's time for you to come out of the darkness. It is time to experience a life of health, wholeness, and joy. It is time for you to rise again, take a deep breath, and then pay it forward by sharing what you learn with others whose lives suck in that very moment. I shall rise again. You will too.

RESURGAM!

TRAUMA CREATES CHANGE
YOU DON'T CHOOSE.
HEALING IS ABOUT CREATING
CHANGE YOU DO CHOOSE.

MICHELE ROSENTHAL, TRAUMA COACH

ONE

CRASH AND BURN

Standing in the middle of a cold, damp country road in a coastal town of England on a grey and drizzly early morning, I was alone and shivering in the chill air. There was silence all around. Not even the birds could be heard. As I breathed, I could see the mist escaping from my mouth as if it were caught by the early morning breeze and carried away. I stood and waited for what seemed like an eternity as the sun began to rise. It broke through the trees along the roadside, so I tried to position myself in such a way that the bright rays would rest on my face to warm me up, even a little bit. My toes were numb, so I stamped my feet on the road to shake life into them and to try to keep moving, yet staying in the same spot. The road was on a slight hill, and I was halfway up it. As I looked up I saw a high steel bridge towering above me. Then I looked down by my feet to see bright red blood trickling down the hill away from "him." His lifeless body lay on the chilly, wet road. I so desperately wanted to lay him on a blanket and cover him up with another one to keep him warm, but I didn't have any with me. What good would it do anyway? He was dead. But it would have made me feel better to be able to do that for him.

He'd tied a rope to the bridge to hang himself, but the rope had unraveled with his weight as he threw himself off the bridge, and he fell to the road below. I was the first officer on the day shift to be sent to the scene to relieve the night shift and to guard the body until SOCO, the British police Scenes of Crime Officers, had gathered the evidence they needed. Only then could appropriate steps be taken for him to be removed. The road had been closed to traffic and pedestrians so no one could come through and contaminate any evidence at the scene.

I never forget a face, and his is permanently etched in my memory. As I watched the blood trickle down the road, I was aware of life leaking out of him. He was staring into the distance, eyes wide open as if fixed in shock and horror. It was creepy to look at his face. I wanted to close his eyes for him but didn't. They were a lovely sky blue, but without life. He was an older man with white hair. At any moment I expected him to twitch, or move, or say something, but he didn't. He just lay there, motionless. Dead.

What was his story? Where was his family? How were they going to receive this tragic news, and who'd be there to help them cope with their grief? Why had he wanted to die? Could anything have been done to save him? Could I pray for him to be raised from the dead? Too many questions to answer. Yet, I kept trying to answer them because it kept my mind focused on cognitive rather than emotional things. I was struck at how upset I really was at the thought of this man dying this way. How can someone be in so much emotional pain and feel so alone and helpless that they make this choice? If only I'd have met him sooner, maybe I could have done something to help. Maybe I could have made a difference.

⊰ ೞ ೞ ೞ ⊱

Mum was a physical therapist and Dad was a police officer in Zambia. One year after they married, I was born in Lusaka hospital, in Zambia, the daughter of parents who were both committed to caring for and serving others. I didn't fall far from that tree; it explains my strong sense of justice and wanting to help those in need.

By the time I was eight, we'd moved to England, and I'd been sent to a boarding school in Norfolk. It was a school for just girls, and I lived at the school, 24/7, only going home to see my family for the summer, Christmas or Easter breaks, plus one week during each twelve-week term, which was called half term. Boarding schools are common in England, and my school days were fun and full of activity. I was often the one that others would come to if they felt lost, lonely, or afraid. Sometimes, if a classmate didn't have any family nearby to go home to during half term, I'd invite them to my house. I loved to be friendly and supportive to others. Even then, it seems, I was passionate about self-care, emotional health, and well-being. Being sent away to school at such a young age made me stand up for myself, be fiercely independent, and it taught me that if I wanted things out of life, I had to make them happen.

My brother, Gus, had been sent to a separate boarding school just for boys when he was six. So, we were raised primarily by our school teachers and the matrons of our dormitories. The other school children became our siblings.

I was happy at school, but I always wondered why I had to be a boarder rather than go daily if my parents only lived about thirty minutes away. I know that they made the choice to send Gus and I away to private schools because they wanted to give us the very best education, and in the UK, most of the best education is found in private schools, such as boarding schools. But why board? Why couldn't we both go home daily and live as a family? I always struggled with that. But, they had their reasons for those decisions and made choices, in their opinions, that were in our best interest. They did what any caring parents do, which is to do their utmost to provide what they believe is the best for their children, and I love them for that. But what they didn't know was that those choices caused me to feel alone when I needed someone's shoulder to cry on or when I needed a hug. Being separated from them taught me not to rely on them or go to them for help or advice. I learned to stand on my own two feet instead. I could trust only my close school friends and myself. So in a way, boarding school life stoked my passion for justice—caring for the underdog, keeping the peace, and bringing emotional healing to hurt and wounded people. I grew up to be tough, self-sufficient, protective of my friends, proactive to get stuff done, caring, loving, and nurturing. Oh, and I also learned to entertain myself when I felt lonely, so I'm now the one who'll plan the fun times, the crazy adventures, and the parties!

When I was twenty I married my husband, Rob, and became a stay at home Mum. Shortly after our last son was born I became a police officer. We were still in England then. I loved police work because it allowed me to serve others in desperate situations. It felt good to be able to help victims of crimes or tragedies, and I also loved the opportunity to share hope, kindness, and encouragement to those we arrested. My heart broke for many of them because they saw so little value in themselves, yet I saw them through different eyes, Jesus's eyes. Eyes that could see them doing well in life if only they could change some of their choices or circumstances. Eyes that were filled with love and compassion for them. I felt sorry for some of them because they were so lost, trapped in a world of self-hate, fears, self-doubt, and addictions. I tried to show them that they mattered by talking to them kindly and encouraging them to get help and stop their lives of crime and destruction in the hope that they'd realize their self-worth and then, in turn, actually believe they could change.

My policing methods were gentler than those of most of my peers, especially the men I worked with, so I was often teased for being too soft. That was their opinion, and they were entitled to that, but personally, I knew I was being true to who I was and what my calling was. I was determined to demonstrate the love of Jesus with all those I came in to contact with and to treat others with respect, no matter if they were the officer I worked with, the witness or victim of a crime, or the suspect I arrested. In my opinion, all people were to be treated kindly and with respect unless they respond to my respect for them in ways that are rude and offensive. In that case, as an officer, I changed my approach as needed to gain control of the situation, make the arrest if necessary and get the job done.

However, the gentle and compassionate side of me was easy to injure. Not due to how people treated me, I could handle that, but due to the stress of the job and the nasty things I had to deal with as a police officer. How can humanity be so cruel? The things I experienced in my short time as an officer had a very negative impact on me. Despite being told during police training that we'd see and hear horrid things, no training can truly prepare you for the things you have to deal with and see as a cop. I saw things I never imagined I'd see. I heard things I hoped I'd never have had to hear. I experienced a side of humanity that was disgusting, degrading, even inhuman at times, it seemed. I saw what people could do to each other and themselves, such as the man who fell from the bridge. I went into homes that shocked me when I saw how some people lived, often through no fault of their own. Each of those experiences chipped away, more and more, at my principles, values, and my belief in the human race. They also rammed against my private school upbringing that was safe, secure, and protected from the real world until I was in my teens.

How naive I was in so many ways! I quickly learned that the "other" world, the world I wasn't raised in, is often messy, destructive, and filled with pain. Those things were all taking their toll on me, but I didn't know it then. On top of that, unbeknown to me, I was struggling with acute physical stress caused by exhaustion. Our police station had a terrible rotating shift pattern that included no less than five shift changes within every six-week cycle. Ranging from early shifts to night shifts and everything in between. We literally had to work a different shift each week. My body just couldn't find its rhythm. Not being able to have a healthy sleeping schedule due to the constant rotating shifts slowly sapped energy from my mind, emotions, body, and spirit. Having four young, active boys who didn't know the meaning of the request, "Please play quietly while I try to sleep," when I was on nights compounded things. Trying to run the household, be a good Mum, and be a good officer was one thing. Trying to sleep during the day, especially when they were out of school, was another. Rob also had a highly stressful job, an hour away from home, so he wasn't available to help with the children most of the time. We rarely asked friends to help because our belief was that they were our children, our responsibility, so it's up to one of us to be with them at all times—even though I desperately needed to sleep. It was always so much easier when Rob was home, but that was rare.

As time went on, I became more exhausted and began to notice some physical, mental, and emotional changes. I ignored them and pushed through because that's what I'd learned to do at school. *No one is here to help me. No one cares, so toughen up and do your job.* I couldn't put my finger on what was going on within me or what caused it, but I just knew something was "off." I began to get terrible migraines that no medication would help. After several weeks of migraines, I noticed that I only had them when I did a particular shift. It was the shift that caused me to get less sleep than the other shifts, so the fatigue put extra stress on my body, which in turn was causing the headaches. After a while, the migraines were so bad that I couldn't work some of my shifts. That, in turn, caused

I COULDN'T PUT MY FINGER ON WHAT WAS GOING ON WITHIN ME OR WHAT CAUSED IT, BUT I JUST KNEW SOMETHING WAS "OFF."

my colleagues to think less of me because it looked as if I wasn't a team player, but no one understood what medical issues I was going through. Not even me. I began to feel like a failure at work.

It wasn't long before I was summoned to the Inspector's office. He'd noticed that I wasn't working all of my shifts and that those I missed were always at the same time. He thought I did that to avoid dealing with some of the more difficult calls we typically responded to on that particular shift, such as the drunken brawls that were

WHAT TO DO WHEN LIFE SUCKS

common when the clubs emptied onto the city streets. Those were actually some of the easier calls, but it doesn't matter now. Based on the pattern of sick days I took off, I can see why he may have thought that. I can also see why that would have been an issue if it were true, but I was mortified that he thought I was avoiding my job due to a lack of courage! But, how do you stand in front of your Inspector and tell him you're not well whenever you work a certain shift due to the lack of sleep, which caused chronic migraines? It did sound ludicrous, and I couldn't explain why that was happening to me because I really didn't understand it all, but that was the reality I faced.

I felt accused, misunderstood, lonely, sick, exhausted, physically weak, and didn't know what to do about it, or that I needed help. Now I had to prove that I wasn't what the inspector thought I was … a coward! Added to that, as a female officer, I believed I had to fight harder, run faster, get more arrests and generally be tougher than the male officers, just to prove that I could do the job and that I deserved to wear the uniform, but I failed in those too. That just wasn't my policing style. The fear of "What is wrong with me?" strengthened and self-condemnation began to take its toll. Still, I pulled up my big-girl panties, toughened up, and pushed through for several more weeks. Fears of failure, cowardice, and the strongest of all, shame, were constantly propelling me forward.

Things got worse, not only mentally as I struggled with the shame and fear of potential failure, but also physically. I started noticing dizzy spells. I was convinced that if I showed my weakness by talking to any other officers about things, even my closest friends, that they'd see me as I saw myself.

The exhaustion continued, and I needed to process some of the difficult calls I'd been on, but that wasn't the culture in our department. There wasn't time to process. We just went from call to call, then to do reports, then home, and back again the next day to do it all again. I finally decided to ask for help and plucked up the courage to speak to my sergeant about it all. I didn't know what help I needed or what could be done for that matter, but I just had to tell someone that I was struggling. It was as if I was fighting an enemy I couldn't see. My sergeant didn't help. I was just told that everyone on our shift faced the same difficulties and that I needed to push through and be a team player. So, I did. Once again I pulled my big-girl panties up, even higher, toughened up even more, and pushed through for several more weeks. But as each shift passed, I noticed myself feeling detached from my colleagues, detached from the job, and unable to focus on anything. I'd lost my passion, my compassion, and my desire even to go work. That saddened me because I'd loved being an officer. It didn't make any sense to me at all. What was wrong with me?

I always patrolled alone, but one morning our shift had just finished our early morning briefing when a call came in for a burglary in progress. Our sergeant told us to partner up for this, so I was partnered with a colleague, who I'll just call D, to locate the suspect. Other officers responded, too, to cover all roads on all sides of the address we'd been given. D and I were patrolling down an alley behind the location to make sure the suspect didn't escape that way. Paying careful attention as I drove, I scanned the many smaller passageways leading to and from the alley to the houses on the right, and D scanned those on the left. We didn't want to miss seeing the suspect down one of those passageways. Suddenly, out of nowhere, a small boy on a bike came flying out of one of the side streets to our left. I slammed on the brakes as hard as I could, but he still hit the side of our patrol car and disappeared from my view. I was devastated! I began feeling physically sick and started shaking, crying, and went numb. I didn't want to get out of the car for fear of seeing his little body lying on the side of the street badly injured, or worse, dead. But adrenaline kicked in, and before I knew it I was out of the car running around to the little boy as D was helping him up. Thankfully he was totally fine other than a bump on his head, and his bike was damaged.

We walked him home and told his parents what had happened. All thoughts of the burglary instantly pushed out of our minds. I was relaying the events that took place and apologized, trying to be the professional police officer, British stiff upper lip, and all that stuff, but I broke, and the tears came. I felt embarrassed that I was in uniform, crying like a baby in front of my partner and the boy's parents. I couldn't believe I'd hit a child! D was kind and encouraging, and the boy's parents were more embarrassed about the fact that their son had ridden his bike out into the street into the path of a police car than they were concerned about his well-being. But I was a mess. D drove the car back to the station, and my sergeant was kind enough to make me a cup of tea. He really did care about me in that moment and asked how I was doing. But, because I had already tried to approach him before to ask for help without any success, the trust in that relationship had been broken, so I shut down. I told him I was fine and pulled myself up by my bootstraps even harder than before!

A few weeks later I got to work and went to the ladies' locker room to put my uniform on. As soon as I had my uniform on, I physically

> I FELT EMBARRASSED THAT I WAS IN UNIFORM, CRYING LIKE A BABY IN FRONT OF MY PARTNER AND THE BOY'S PARENTS

started to shake—just as I had done when I hit the little boy. I didn't know what was going on, but I felt very weak, close to tears, and my brain was so foggy that I couldn't think straight. I went to the report writing room to finish some reports left over from my last shift and logged into the computer, but my eyes couldn't focus on the computer screen. When I put my fingers on the keyboard to type, my hands shook so much, and my whole body started tingling. I couldn't type or focus on the words on the screen. It felt so strange. I thought I was going to collapse. I had to get help. Instead of going to my sergeant again, or to the Inspector, I went to the Chief Inspector. I felt so guilty that I was going behind my sergeant's back to ask for help after he'd already told me just to pull it together. I was worried that I'd be disciplined for doing so, but I knew I needed help, and I knew that the Chief Inspector was a kind, gentle, and understanding man who listened well. He immediately put me at ease. As I explained what was going on and described my symptoms he immediately seemed to understand what I needed. He told me to go home, take some time off and make an appointment as soon as possible with the police surgeon. I felt instant relief, mixed with shame, guilt, and embarrassment. Suddenly I'd become one of "those."

The police surgeon was one of only a handful of police doctors in the country at that time. He was assigned to work both as a forensic physician, examining offenders and victims of crime, and also as an occupational health advisor, looking after the welfare of the force's staff. Thank goodness he knew what my problem was. He told me it was stress-related and said that I should take some extended time off and get rest, really rest. Thank goodness for his wisdom. However, that came with its own set of problems because I was in a police force that mocked "those" who had gone off with "stress-related" issues. They were always talked about in the break room as the weaklings, those that crashed and burned, or "those" that didn't deserve to be "in the job." People who went off with stress weren't trusted on the team to have their comrades' backs, so now I was one of those people that other cops talked about negatively. I was now the loser on our shift. My struggle with guilt, shame, embarrassment, and a total sense of being the outcast made my already weakened, acutely stressed, and exhausted self, feel far worse.

I had crashed and burned but still fought the lies, the emotional baggage, and accusations that ran around my head, telling me that I was a loser and that everyone knew it. I believed they were right.

I ended up not being able to work for six months. Those six months were a blur to me. Partly because I was on anti-depressants and partly because I was so unwell that I barely remember anything other than being curled up on the floor in my living room by the wall heater trying to keep warm and crying. I didn't have the energy to see anyone, to cook meals for our family, or to clean the house. Rob was amazing and stepped up in every area that he could. I just sat in silence and battled with the guilt and shame of not being at work. I cried because I felt so exhausted and useless, and then I cried because I felt guilty about not being with my fellow officers. I desperately wanted to be a team player, not to be the loser or the officer that let my colleagues down by causing them to be short-handed on shift. I knew how much work everyone already had on their plates, and now, because of me, they also had to carry my load. Yet the thought of actually going on duty made me start shaking again, and I knew I couldn't do it. My brain battled against my emotions and my will, which in turn negatively affected my body physically.

At no time in that six months was I ever offered any further help or support from the police department. My supervisors didn't check on me; most of my shift colleagues didn't come to visit me. I was out of sight and out of mind. I felt ignored, abandoned, and was left believing that I was the problem. In those days in England, we didn't have police chaplains or peer support teams as we do here in America. So, I was told to take Prozac for six months and stay home to rest. That in itself wasn't a bad thing because I did need to rest, and the Prozac did help to numb my emotions, but no one helped me to address what had caused my acute stress or my inability to do my job in the first place. No one helped me to learn how to do it better when I went back.

After about four months, I got a letter from the police force telling me that unless I returned to work within a certain time frame, they'd stop my pay. Other than that, and a couple of police friends checking in on me, I had no contact from the police force for which I worked. Nothing. At some point I saw a counselor for a few weeks, and that did help.

Eventually, I had to go back to work before I was fully ready because we needed the money, and the police force would only pay for a few months of sick leave, no matter if my issues were job-related or not. When I returned to work, I was again faced with the shame that I'd been one of those loser officers who couldn't cut it. My position in my old team had been filled by another officer, which I totally understood, because the job still had to be done. I was put on light duties, mainly office work, until I was ready to go on patrol again. I was on my own in an office on a different shift under a different sergeant. It was hard to go to work every day feeling as if I'd let the team down, believing that I was the weakest link and sensing the sideways comments that I didn't deserve to wear the uniform because I wasn't strong enough to cope with the job.

WHAT TO DO WHEN LIFE SUCKS

Each time I go back home to England to visit friends and family, my mind quickly recalls horrific memories of certain calls for service that I had at various addresses where I lived and worked. As I drive around, I'm often triggered by images and sounds of the things I saw and experienced, like the bridges that people jumped off. When I drive over them to this day, some 20 years later, it still causes me to go silent as I remember the victims' names, stories, and faces. Then there are the roads where lives were lost in crashes and the houses that kept dark secrets of murder or abuse. Sometimes I cry, sometimes I shudder, and occasionally I even smile at a good memory. The memories are not always bad, but the bad ones certainly outweigh the good ones.

I know that if I'd had the right support, things would have been very different. I may not have crashed and burned because I'd have had somewhere to go for help and may not have hit rock bottom so hard. I believe I'd have made a full recovery and had a fulfilling career, but that wasn't the case. I'd gone back to work too soon, back into the same toxic environment and on the same awful rotating shifts, and they soon began to retake their toll. Sadly, it wasn't too long before I walked away from the career I loved. Wounded, lost, and broken. Not knowing where and how to get the help I needed to heal fully. But God knew...

I KNOW THAT IF I'D HAD THE RIGHT SUPPORT, THINGS WOULD HAVE BEEN VERY DIFFERENT.

It wasn't long before we moved to the US and settled in California. There I was fortunate enough to be invited to volunteer at a local police department in the investigations department and dispatch. Being back in a police environment without the shift work did me a lot of good. My soul was slowly healing, my confidence grew, and I began to feel stronger again, with a new sense of purpose. I was acutely aware of a deep passion within me to do all that I could to make sure that these officers and other first responders didn't crash and burn, like I did, so I took several courses on various aspects of psychological trauma and disaster response. I'd found my niche!

For the next ten years, my work focused on helping people in emotional distress. First responders and civilians alike.

The compassion I had for my school friends who needed a friend; the questions I struggled with on the cold Suffolk road with the man who fell from the bridge; the drive to ensure that first responders don't crash and burn like I did; the deep inner desires to help people in emotional pain from a very young age all revealed my God-designed destiny that I didn't recognize until years later. With God, nothing is wasted. Ever.

All of the traumatic experiences I've been through personally, the desperate grief, the shock, the many times I've screamed out with emotional pain and walked through valleys of darkness, only to come out the other side fitter, stronger, wiser and healthier than before, have all made me into the person I am today. The skills and experience I possess give me the humble privilege of being a trauma responder to people in emotional distress, both nationally and internationally, a chaplain to both first responders and civilians, an international speaker and instructor, and now an author. I will share with you what I have learned so that you don't have to crash and burn, and if you already have, to be encouraged that you can rise again. ***RESURGAM!***

YOU DON'T HAVE TO
CRASH AND BURN LIKE I
DID, AND IF YOU ALREADY
HAVE, BE ENCOURAGED—
YOU CAN RISE AGAIN.

WHAT WOULD JESUS DO?

By now, you have learned that I'm passionate about emotional health and overall well-being for everyone. Yes, that means you too. I'm eager to help you to become more aware of how God designed your body, mind, soul, and emotions to respond naturally to the stressful seasons you'll experience in your life. Especially the overwhelmingly crippling ones. We've never been promised an easy life. Bad stuff happens to people of all faiths, from all social groups in society, all cultures, and countries. So, it's not a matter of if, but when something hits you so hard that you have the wind knocked out of your sails, causing you to veer off course for a while. Some of you may even hit the ground, but that is never the end of your story! I hope you'll find some useful strategies in this book to help you take deep breaths, and to stabilize yourself until you're able to refocus and get your feet firmly under you again. On your new firm ground of knowledge, understanding, right choices, and great support, you'll be able to push yourself onwards and upwards—you shall rise again—walking into a stronger, healthier, and more stable future. I'm eager for you to have a better understanding of what emotional health really means and to empower you to be more proactive about your own self-care. Your mental and emotional health depends on your self-care, which enables you to manage daily stress and have useful coping mechanisms to navigate the challenges that arise during and after a seriously critical event.

When you have endured something painful and difficult and have been able to overcome the trial, you emerge wiser and stronger. Rising again in victory gives you credibility to help someone else through a similar experience. Your wisdom and first-hand knowledge qualify you to hold the next person's hand and support them in their hour of need.

Jesus has that victory. The cross provides His credibility. He was crushed, bruised, murdered, and then buried in a tomb for three days, but He overcame that traumatic, evil experience. He had His own Resurgam moment and rose again more powerful and even deadlier to the enemy, Satan, than anyone could imagine. He loves us so much that by example, He lived the way He wants us to. He lovingly leads us through our trials so that from His experience and by His authority that He gives us, we too can rise again to overcome. He turns to help us in our hour of need so we can experience our own Resurgam destiny.

I wonder if some of you are about to cast this book aside and stop reading it right here. You may be telling yourself that Jesus didn't go through what you're going through, so He doesn't understand the pain you're in. You may tell yourself that He never faced the suicide of a family member; He was never raped or sexually abused. Jesus didn't have to deal with losing a house and all of his belongings in a fire, nor did He lose a spouse in a car crash or a child to a drug overdose. He wasn't treated badly by his family or friends, nor did He grow old and suffer sickness and disease like cancer or any other terminal illness.

You may even be thinking that because He is Jesus, He has more power and authority than you do to overcome life's challenges. Perhaps you feel that because He was both God and man, any hardships He faced weren't as traumatic as they are for you. After all, He is all-powerful, isn't He? Couldn't He just use His power to pick Himself up every time and keep on going? It is difficult for us to think of Jesus as ever showing signs of grief or stress or trauma, but just the opposite is true.

Let me take you on a quick journey to explore Jesus' life to see some of the most painful things any human could bear.

GRIEF

Scripture records that when Jesus heard the news of his beloved cousin, John the Baptist, being brutally murdered by beheading, He withdrew. He left the disciples and the multitudes behind, got into a boat, and sought a solitary, private place. He didn't just go for a walk down the road to get away from those around Him; He put a lot of distance between Himself and people. He went across some water to find a solitary place away from everyone. Why would He do that? Because He's in shock and is grieving. He's just been given some tragic news about John, who was probably more like a brother to Jesus than just a cousin. He lost a family member He loved dearly.

If bad news doesn't affect you, there's no need to have privacy, no need to find a solitary place. When you've heard bad news, have you withdrawn? I most certainly have, and it's always because I can't handle my emotions in public. Because they're so strong, I need privacy to allow myself to express them freely. I'm confident that even though it's not explained here, Jesus needed privacy to cry and grieve the loss of His beloved cousin. He felt the pain of grief—the anger and rage caused by the injustice of John's murder. He experienced what it was like to lose a loved one to a violent death. That's very traumatic for Jesus. Not only is He struggling with grief, but the added pain that this wasn't a natural death. It was murder!

JESUS FELT THE PAIN OF GRIEF— HE KNEW WHAT IT WAS LIKE TO LOSE A LOVED ONE TO A VIOLENT DEATH.

When you lose a loved one due to natural causes, or a gradual death caused by illness, there's usually time for everyone to say their goodbyes and share their hearts with one another before the death takes place. People tend to have time in those situations to begin to process through the knowledge that death will take place. I'm not saying that it makes it easier to lose a loved one if you know they're dying. Still, in my personal and professional experience, when dealing with a violent death, like a murder or suicide, the loss is often more painful because it's sudden and unexpected. Premature death is often shrouded in many unanswered questions such as why? What happened? Who would do this? Or why didn't they come to me for help? Those questions can make the death far more painful, more traumatic to deal with because there's less closure, no answers in which to find comfort. A tragic or untimely death is often met with anger in the loved ones left behind. That's what Jesus experienced too. He's been there, done that, and has the experience to help you with that kind of pain too.

BETRAYAL

Have any of you felt the disbelief, the numbing, deep wounds of betrayal? Jesus has too. *"After Jesus had said these things, He was troubled (disturbed, agitated) in spirit and said, I assure you, most solemnly I tell you, one of you will deliver Me up [one of you will be false to Me and betray Me]!"*[1] Here it clearly describes Jesus's emotional state. He was disturbed and agitated. I think that's putting it mildly! One of his own disciples, Judas Iscariot, is about to betray him—to death—and Jesus knew it. Can you imagine the pain of betrayal from a close friend? Sure, many of you can. It's very painful. Here, Jesus knows he is going to die and a friend set it up! Talk about being stabbed in the back—literally. Have you been betrayed? Jesus can help you through that pain.

REJECTION

Let's look at the pain of rejection and abandonment. We've all felt rejected or abandoned at some point, but in this passage, Jesus was pushed out of Nazareth, His home town where He was raised. He had just finished teaching in the synagogue:

> *When they heard these things, all the people in the synagogue were filled with rage. And rising up, **they pushed and drove Him out of the town,** and [laying hold of Him] they led Him to the [projecting] upper part of the hill on which their town was*

built, that they might hurl Him headlong down [over the cliff].
But passing through their midst, He went on His way.²

I can't imagine what it must be like to be spurned like this, but I've certainly felt unwanted in many ways. The feelings of being unwanted cut so deep because we're all designed to be in relationship. We all thrive on belonging, on being loved. When we experience the opposite of that, it cuts to the core of our being and hurts deeply. But we can rise again from that pit of pain and heal thanks to Jesus. But look closely, they also planned to murder Jesus, too, by throwing Him off the cliff. It says He passed through their midst and went on His way, which seems very tame. The reality is more likely that He fought for His life and managed to escape.

Just before Jesus died, He'd been imprisoned and was despised. At the cross, Jesus was mocked, stripped naked, beaten, ridiculed, tortured, and scorned. He took all of our sickness and diseases upon Himself. He was exhausted. Weak. Traumatized emotionally, mentally, and physically and was ultimately murdered by His own people, the Jews. Don't you think He went through enough to understand our pain, our torment, our trauma? Absolutely! He experienced it all and more so than many of us.

Even though I have shared some passages to describe some of the struggles Jesus faced as a human being, there's still much more. Read this passage and see how many of the highlighted words describe the pain and suffering He went through when He died for us—not just physically but emotionally too.

*He was **despised** and **rejected** and **forsaken** by men, a Man of **sorrows** and **pains**, and **acquainted with grief and sickness**; and like One from Whom men hide their faces He was **despised**, and we did not appreciate His worth or have any* *esteem for Him. Surely He has borne our *__griefs (sicknesses,__ __weaknesses, and distresses)__ and carried our __sorrows and__ __pains [of punishment]__, yet we [ignorantly] considered Him __stricken, smitten, and afflicted__ by God [as if with leprosy]. But He was __wounded__ for our transgressions; He was __bruised__ for our guilt and iniquities; the __chastisement__ [needful to obtain] peace and well-being for us was upon Him, and with the __stripes__ __[that wounded] Him__ we are healed and made whole.³*

∾❧ ೞ ೞ ೞ ❧∾

Throughout this book, I'll reference some translations from the original Hebrew language in which the Old Testament was written as well as Greek translations for the New Testament. I use *Strong's Concordance* for this to research the original meaning of words to get a clearer picture of what is being said. In Isaiah's passage, the Hebrew translation of the word *griefs* is diseases, afflictions, sadness, distresses, an evil, or a calamity. Those are strong words and not words that we'd usually associate with the word grief. Yet, it's clear that Jesus experienced all of those emotions and symptoms, just as we do when troubles come our way. So, He's more than qualified to guide us through our own troubles.

We know that Jesus experienced much turmoil in the three short years between beginning his ministry and dying, but have you ever wondered how awful it must be to go through as much pain and loss, betrayal, and rejection as that in such a short period of time? Then to cap it all off, he died for us! Thanks to His sacrifice and victory, we can be healed of all sickness and disease—mentally, emotionally, physically, behaviorally, and spiritually. Like Him, we can rise again from the ashes of pain and trauma and experience well-being, health, and wholeness. Our job is to then do the same for others by bringing His message of Good News to those that are suffering. Paying it forward, so to speak.

BRINGING GOOD NEWS

In Luke, Jesus encourages us by telling us that when we go through very stressful and even traumatic times, He has provided a way for us to overcome those challenges.

> *The Spirit of the Lord [is] upon Me, because He has anointed Me [the Anointed One, the Messiah] to preach the Good News (the Gospel) to the poor; He has sent Me to announce release to the captives and recovery of sight to the blind, to send forth as delivered those who are oppressed [who are downtrodden, bruised, crushed, and broken down by calamity].* [4]

What's Jesus really saying here? The answers may surprise you. When Jesus says that He's come to preach the Good News to the poor, He's not necessarily telling us that He's standing in a synagogue or on a mountain top preaching to a crowd of people. Although, when He said this, He was, in fact, in the synagogue in Nazareth just before they tried to push him out of town and throw him off the cliff. But He's telling us that generally, as we go about our daily lives and business, we're to keep an eye out for anyone in need of hearing the Good News of the Gospel. In my experience, many people are far more open to hearing that Good News when they're in trauma, desperate, with their backs up against the wall, crying out to God after they've already tried everything else first. This is where you and I can come in and bring the loving, powerful touch of Jesus into their lives. In this passage, Jesus says He's preaching the Good News to the *poor*. Now, we all know that the word poor means not having enough money to live on, possibly being reduced to begging and financial destitution. But the original Greek word here also refers to people being poor in a societal position, helpless, lacking honor, or being powerless to accomplish anything that will make a difference in their circumstances. It also means that they're lacking in their spirit, empty. Here, the word poor refers to mental, emotional, and financial poverty in various ways.

Can you think of times in your life when you've been poor in these ways? What kind of good news helped you to fill that poverty with the riches of hope, encouragement, a lifted spirit, and yes, even financial provision? What about the emotional poverty that people experience after a traumatic event, or after a lifetime of struggles that leave them feeling powerless to change anything, or that leave them feeling dishonored, without any place in society. Can you see how you and I can bring hope to someone by just sharing some good news with them? Good news such as telling them that there are resources available to help them, that they're not alone, and just being with them for a while. When you're willing to sit with someone who feels invisible, it validates and values them and gives them a place in society by acknowledging their existence.

WHEN YOU SIT WITH SOMEONE WHO FEELS INVISIBLE, IT VALIDATES AND VALUES THEM.

RELEASING THE CAPTIVES

The next thing Jesus says is that He came to announce release to the *captives*, which in this biblical context, according to *Strong's Concordance*, means prisoners of war. How can we be prisoners of war if we're at home or working in a safe country that's not even at war?

33

This isn't a literal quote in the usual sense of the phrase that most of us would understand. Still, we do all battle against daily stressors, difficulties, and challenges in life, which can be so overwhelming that our minds, bodies, spirits, and our souls can feel as if we're trapped with no way out. That is a form of being held captive. When we can't see a way out of hardships, we can be held captive, like a prisoner, in the battle in which we find ourselves.

Taking it a step further into the spiritual realm, people can be held captive by spiritual forces, by sickness, and disease. There are so many ways that we're held captive. I'd venture to say that we've all been bound by captivity in one way or another for so long that we're used to it and accept it as being normal, and therefore don't do anything about it. But anything that goes against God's plan for your life or that goes against God's Kingdom principles is far from normal! It blinds you, then binds you and keeps you captive, which means you're not free. You're a slave to whatever binds you, and Jesus came to set the captives free! That is great news! You and I are to do the same thing for others by sharing the truth of His Word, His healing touch, and even His deliverance with those that need it. Bringing healing frees people.

BRINGING SIGHT TO BLIND EYES

The word *blind* in this verse can certainly mean the loss of eyesight because, yes, Jesus does want to heal those who can't see physically, but it also refers to those who are mentally blind. Have you ever felt mentally blind? Think of a time when you've been unable to think straight or mentally process things as you normally would. Or a time when you've not been able to figure out how to deal with difficulties in life or make decisions because you've been unable to focus due to such acute stress, grief, shock, or other emotional trauma. When we can't focus, we don't move because we can't see the way forward. Acute stress can cause this. Some medications can cause it too. Being overwhelmed in any of these areas can cause mental blindness. Still, Jesus came to give sight to the blind, meaning that when life becomes too painful or so emotionally traumatic that we can't figure out what to do or even arrange our jumbled thoughts in any kind of order, He lovingly and gently leads us by showing us the way through our mental fog.

Think of times when you haven't known what to do in a situation. Have you prayed for wisdom and direction? Or have you asked a friend for advice? Either way, when you receive an answer, you have direction. That's what it means to receive sight in an area where you didn't have sight before. Another word for this is insight, meaning that we see *inside* our minds rather than *outside* with our physical eyes. We can do that for other people, too, by holding their hands and guiding them through their traumas, helping them to see the way forward by helping them to find and plug into resources, doctors, therapists, support groups, etc. That is how we can bring recovery of sight to the blind. Just as Jesus does when He saves us, He clearly shows us the way by lighting our paths to salvation. But before that, we were blind to the truth that sets us free.

DELIVERANCE TO THE OPPRESSED

To be *oppressed* means to be bruised, trodden, crushed, or broken down by calamity. Can you think of times when you've felt so crushed, so broken that you can't pick yourself up again and put the pieces of your life back together the way you want to, or when you want to? Those things take time, and we're not always good at trusting that healing process. Jesus promises to deliver us from oppression and heal our bruises. The word *bruise* comes from the Greek word *suntribó,* meaning to break into pieces by crushing or to shatter. Suntribó comes from the same root word from which we get the word *trauma.* Lastly, a *calamity*, according to *Strong's*, is an event that brings terrible loss, lasting distress, or severe affliction such as a disaster or something that brings dire distress resulting from loss or tragedy. Has something so calamitous happened to you that you go into shock for a while? It's happened to me.

∽CʒCʒCʒ∽

Am I going to die? I don't want to die! My mind was racing. Moment by moment passed as I imagined the disease taking over. At least, that is how it felt. My heart ached with sadness and fear.

I'd just had my routine annual mammogram the month before. The report was good, "All is fine; come back next year." But I knew that something was wrong. I asked for some further tests to be done on my right breast. After some forceful self advocation, my doctor finally agreed, saying, "Purely for your own peace of mind," and ordered an ultrasound begrudgingly because she believed mammogram results were accurate. A week later, I had an ultrasound, which prompted the radiologist to recommend a follow-up ultrasound-guided biopsy. Something obviously was not right.

Waiting was horrid! Waiting for the days until the biopsy appointment arrived. Waiting for the biopsy results. Waiting for some sort of information that would allow me to move forward and escape from the frozen space of time in which I felt stuck.

The thoughts that bombarded my mind during those waiting days were relentless ... remembering my mother's traumatic death to cancer that ravaged her body and slowly squeezed out all life and breath from her in a most painful and ugly way. I had terrible images of her in my head. She'd died just two years earlier, and those images haunted me. Convinced that this was going to be how my life ended, too, the fear that filled me was so overwhelming that I began to retreat into isolation. I didn't want to see people, talk to people, or be asked countless questions about how I was doing. So, I hid and avoided everyone.

After the biopsy the following week, my anxiety increased. I was waiting yet again—this time for a life or death phone call. You are cancer free; you'll live! Or, you have cancer; you might die. Every time the phone rang, my heart skipped a beat as I felt adrenalin dump into my system, causing my heart to race with apprehension. I'd hesitate for a brief moment, taking a deep breath before checking the caller ID on my screen. It was as if I was putting distance, or time, between myself and the news I was expecting and dreading simultaneously. I'd let out a huge sigh, relieving the immediate stress built up inside me, force a big smile on my face, and say with false joy, "Hello, this is Fran ..." Some of you know what I mean. You've been there!

After a few days had passed and I'd not heard from the doctor, I began to relax, figuring that no news was good news. My erratic emotions had begun to calm down, and I was actually feeling more positive and happier. Rob and I took a four-hour drive from our home to go to a party in the Bay area. We were looking forward to a fun evening with good friends and had arranged to stay in a hotel for the night, a mini-retreat. It felt so good to get out of the house, get away for a little adventure, and escape from the reality I left behind at home. I needed a "normal" day again. On the way to the party, we stopped to get gas. While I waited in the car for Rob to pump the gas, I wondered again why I'd not heard back from the doctor. I sensed an inner strength and courage rise in me, which gave me the confidence to phone the doctor to see if he had heard anything from the pathologists. I wanted to confirm what I was beginning to believe—that I was cancer-free.

Numbness, silence, everything stopped. I put down the phone, turned to face Rob, and heard the words come out of my mouth, seemingly spoken by a stranger. "I have cancer." Even as I said those words, it was as if I was just reciting the lines of a play—a play about a life that wasn't mine. I felt strangely calm in that moment as if I was in a bubble ... nothing inside that bubble was real, but I couldn't step out of it back into the real world that I'd been in a few seconds earlier. The world around me literally melted into slow motion. The entire conversation I just had with the doctor seemed to be about somebody else, not me. I was in shock but don't remember any real emotion other than just being very matter of fact and controlled as I discussed the facts with my doctor. It was as if we'd discussed someone else's diagnosis, not mine.

THE WORLD AROUND ME LITERALLY MELTED INTO SLOW MOTION ... I WAS IN SHOCK ...

Then, suddenly I felt fear, confusion, anger, and also an intense desire to fight this, all rising up in me at the same time. I had to stop this disease before it stopped me. I felt driven to take control of the situation ... but it was out of my control. For the very first time in my life, there was absolutely nothing I could do. I had to face this new journey head-on, pull up my big-girl panties, and walk forward through the unfamiliar, uncertain, daunting doors open before me.

Rob and I didn't have much time to talk about all this; by now, we'd almost arrived at the party. We wanted to have fun, enjoy the evening and turn back the clock to a time when I hadn't spoken to the doctor. We decided to deal with this later, so we put forced smiles on our faces, lied through our teeth, and pretended everything was normal. Inside I was screaming, fighting back the tears, and exhausted from all of the strength it took me to hold everything in and be "happy" all evening. I had to stuff it back in "the cupboard," knowing I would have to take it out again when I was ready to face it. In reality, I wanted to lock that cupboard door and throw away the bloody key! How could anyone be "ready" to face a diagnosis of cancer and pretend everything was okay? Who was I kidding! I felt poor in spirit because I suddenly felt so downtrodden and alone even though I was surrounded by people who cared for me. I felt emotionally crushed, bruised, and terrified. I was mentally blind because I couldn't think straight. In a blink of an eye, my whole world was turned upside down, and I didn't know where to turn or which way was up. I was numb with shock and had been taken captive by the news of my cancer diagnosis, not only physically but also mentally and emotionally.

⚜ ❧❦ ⚜

Cancer was my enemy, and I had a huge fight to face, and I felt all of the symptoms and conditions described in Luke 4:18 & 19. How was Jesus going to make that verse come true for me? I really believed

I was going to die and didn't know how this scripture would apply to me. By going through this scary and traumatic illness, plus other painful life experiences, those answers did come. Not only did I rise again and learn even more about the effects of trauma, but I also learned how to help others through the pain so that they could rise again too. *RESURGAM!*

Endnotes

1. John 13:21.

2. Luke 4:28-30.

3. Isaiah 53:3-5.

4. Luke 4:18-19.

THREE

WHAT MAKES AN EVENT TRAUMATIC?

There's a big difference between feeling stressed and being in emotional or psychological trauma, but the term "stressed" has become a bit of a buzz word, both for someone who's being moody or for someone who's traumatized. We all feel certain levels of stress each day. This is normal and not always a bad thing as I'll explain later. However, negative stress shouldn't always be taken as lightly as it is. Acute stress or trauma is serious because, if ignored, it can lead to dysfunction. Acute stress, trauma, and dysfunction are all different levels of distress, which can be caused by one major traumatic event and is otherwise referred to as a critical or traumatic incident. Some examples are a serious terminal medical diagnosis, the death of a loved one, loss of a job, a disaster or tragedy. Distress can also be caused by compounded events, such as ongoing abuse, enduring fighting in a war, or continuing repeated stressful events. These ongoing events may not necessarily be as traumatic as one sudden major trauma; however, the fact that you have to deal with ongoing taxing events can slowly build up your stress levels over time. At some point, this leads to feeling overwhelmed, and then one day, something else happens, and it's the last straw—you break. To get an idea of what causes acute distress or emotional trauma, let's first look at the definition of a disaster and see how a disaster affects a city as an example.

Disasters can be sudden onset or slow onset. Sudden onset disasters can happen without warning and are so powerful that they cause great destruction and possibly death. An example of a natural, sudden onset disaster is a severe earthquake, flash flood, tornado, tsunami, or other weather-related event. Disasters can also be man-made, such as an act of terrorism or war, a mass shooting, or arson, which causes overwhelming wildland fires. A slow onset disaster is more like the unfolding of a pandemic, a disease outbreak, or mass starvation, which evolves and wreaks havoc over time.

According to FEMA (the Federal Emergency Management Agency), a disaster is a **critical event** that seriously disrupts the functioning of a large group of people, such as a city. This means that a disaster exceeds the impacted city's ability to cope with the event because it overwhelms the city's resources, such as their police departments, fire departments, first responders, hospitals, utility workers, plus others. When this happens, the city relies heavily on what's called Mutual Aid, which is a previously agreed upon contract with outside resources and agencies that agree to come into the city to help cover all of the needs that the city can't manage itself. Such as, extra police coming to help patrol the streets, guard blockades, keep people out of unsafe areas, or to deal with the increased crime that can occur following disasters. It may include things like extra medical staff from hospitals in neighboring cities that may come to support overwhelmed hospital staff, or extra fire departments coming in with more equipment because the city's equipment may have been damaged or there just aren't enough fire engines and medical vehicles to manage the increased needs. In a nutshell, the city isn't able to manage the impact of the disaster without outside help, to regain control, to protect its people, and to establish order and bring life back to normal; it relies on outside resources to recover.

Keep that example in your mind as we look at a critical incident or traumatic event. A critical incident or traumatic event is any event that overwhelms a person's normal coping mechanisms. Just as a disaster is so big for a city that it overwhelms its resources, similarly, a critical or traumatic event is too big, too powerful for a person to cope with, so it overwhelms their coping resources too. These events are often abrupt, unexpected, sometimes life-threatening, and fall outside the range of that person's normal life experiences. Compounded events can have the same effect over time. A critical incident impacts a person so severely that they are unable to rationalize or make sense of what has happened to them. They are unable to process it or "file" the event away mentally or emotionally. Such incidents cause an **acute stress response**, which results in **severe distress**, also known as **emotional or psychological trauma**.

> A CRITICAL INCIDENT OR TRAUMATIC EVENT IS ANY EVENT THAT OVERWHELMS A PERSON'S NORMAL COPING MECHANISMS.

So, the critical or traumatic event is the actual circumstance that took place, which negatively affected the person's coping skills, causing them to be overwhelmed. Their normal and common stress responses to the event can cause them to be "in crisis." We usually say they're in acute distress or experiencing psychological trauma. But, just like a community can't recover without help from outside resources, a person in true acute distress or psychological trauma also needs help from outside resources to recover. This may involve things such as seeing a therapist, attending a support group, receiving care from a network of other friends and family members, seeing a chaplain or pastor or even seeing their doctor and being given some medications temporarily to help with the emotional pain until they can begin to cope again and walk towards recovery.

Examples of Critical Incidents & Traumatic Events:

- Violent crime
- Sexual, physical, verbal, mental, emotional abuse
- Loss of status, security, finances, job, hopes, and dreams
- Serious illness or diagnosis
- Loss of a loved one (death) or relationships (divorce or relocation)
- Death of a pet

WHAT DOES THE TERM PSYCHOLOGICAL TRAUMA ACTUALLY MEAN?

In psychology, the word "psyche" refers to the human mind, both the conscious and subconscious parts. The basic meaning of the Greek word for psyche is *life* in the sense of breath, spirit, or soul.

The word trauma comes from a Greek word meaning a wound. So, when you put the two words together, psyche and trauma, it means wounded soul, wounded spirit, or wounded mind, both the conscious and subconscious parts. Each time we experience something that is so emotionally taxing that it causes grief, shock, distress, trauma, or dysfunction, it cuts away at our soul and wounds us. If you were injured and you could see your wound externally, or you could feel internal pain and discomfort, you'd take steps to help that physical medical issue to heal. If you couldn't manage that at home, you'd see a doctor to get medicine and advice because otherwise your body won't function as it should and your pain would continue. Sometimes that pain is so intense that it actually stops you from being able to move or function normally. What if your injury is so severe that you end up in the ER or are admitted to hospital? Do you think you'd be able to stay home, pretend it's not there and expect it to just go away over time? If you did that, it would get worse, get infected, and you could run the risk of severe illness and death. But because we cannot see our emotional pain or identify a wounded soul, we often ignore that, just like our bodies, it may need assistance to recover.

It's very important to understand that your soul, your inner being, gets wounded too, just as your physical body does. Your soul gets cut, slashed, crushed, and bruised.[1] Trust me, just because you can't see those wounds doesn't mean they're not there. The problem is that they're often ignored because they're invisible, and when that happens, they run the risk of festering. The infection can cause the emotional, subconscious wound in your soul to grow and grow and grow until one day, like

YOUR SOUL SUFFERS TRAUMA AND GETS WOUNDED JUST LIKE YOUR PHYSICAL BODY DOES.

a large blister that gets so big that it bursts, you erupt mentally and emotionally. Just as I crashed and burned in the police force, you run the risk of doing the same due to the result of undealt with traumatic or acutely stressful issues that you've carried over time. Unfortunately, when we've ignored our internal pains and nightmares for so long that we erupt, it tends to happen at the most awful time and can be so messy that it takes longer to recover than we imagine it could. I hope to help you to understand how to pay attention to the internal and external warning signs of accumulative or sudden stress and trauma so that you don't erupt. I want you to pay more attention to your internal, subconscious wounds, just as you do for your physical ones so that your soul is healthy.

> "Now if I do what I do not desire to do, it is no longer I doing it [it is not myself that acts], but the sin [principle] which dwells within me [fixed and operating in my soul]."
>
> Romans 7:20

Don't you just hate it when you behave or respond in such a way that you know is unkind or inappropriate, and you know you have a habit of just reacting that way? No matter how many times you tell yourself to stop or to be nice and not react so badly, your automated response to that same situation is to repeat those behaviors, and you just don't understand why. Yup. We all do that. It's natural, but not necessarily right or healthy. The flip side is that our automated responses could always be kind, compliant, obedient—and those all sound wonderful, and in healthy, safe relationships they are. Yet, there are times when those aren't healthy or appropriate responses because they could lead to abuse and neglect if you have people around who bully you or take you for granted. Even though you know this, you still can't seem to change your responses to stick up for yourself. That is what Paul is referring to in the passage above. I'd like to share some insight that may help.

OUR SOUL IS A FILTER

When trauma wounds our souls, it affects every single area of life because we filter reactions, emotions, and behaviors through our souls. If our souls aren't healthy, our filter system will be clogged with negativity, which results in poor reactions. Imagine the filter in your vacuum cleaner being so clogged because of all of the dirt that it's plugged up with. When it's that dirty, the vacuum doesn't work properly. It loses its suction power and doesn't pick up the dirt from the floor, sometimes pushing dirt back out into the air again. The point of a vacuum cleaner's filter is to stop dust, dirt, and allergens from being released back into the air. The vacuum cycles the air in through its canister to deposit all of the dirt, hair, and particles it collects, and as the air exits the canister, it's pushed through the vacuum filter. The filter catches the dirt, making sure it all stays inside the canister rather than being released into the air again, settling down as another layer of dust in your house. Over time, the filter gets clogged up with so much dust and dirt that it stops working, which is why you have to replace it or clean it regularly. It is the only way your vacuum can keep working effectively and keep your house clean.

Our souls are like the vacuum filter. When they're so plugged with dirt due to our negative life's experiences, they aren't clean and healthy enough to be able to filter things properly, which allows the dirt in our hearts to be released through our thoughts, words, and actions. When that happens, we spray our dirt all over others—especially our loved ones and closest friends. But we shouldn't keep contaminating other people with our negative and dirty stuff. When we've been emotionally wounded in life, either because of our own choices or because others have hurt us, we learn patterns of responses and behaviors due to our inner need and drive to self-protect.

If we're being wounded or hurt mentally and emotionally, our souls are wounded too. As the Romans scripture explains, when we operate from a wounded place and allow our wounded soul to filter our reactions, it can cause us to think wrong thoughts. Which then makes us believe lies about ourselves and the world or people around us. In turn, it impacts our will, causing us to make unhealthy choices, which alters our automatic behavioral responses. Over time, these learned behaviors from past traumas become so natural to us that we think it's just "who we are," but it's not really who Jesus created us to be.

Has it occurred to you that your negative attitudes may be caused by past disappointments and hurts? Did you know that all wounds, if undealt with, can manifest in our bodies as sickness, stiffness, aches and pains, and even chronic disease? If we don't stop the negative filters from controlling our thoughts and actions, we potentially make unhealthy choices and have inappropriate behavior. Each time we choose or behave wrongly, we're not acting according to our heavenly design, meaning that we run the risk of being in sin. That, in turn, wounds our souls again, which causes

> DISAPPOINTMENTS AND SOUL WOUNDS CAN MANIFEST AS SICKNESS IN OUR BODIES, STIFFNESS, ACHES AND PAINS, AND EVEN CHRONIC DISEASE

wrong thinking and wrong behavior. So, we're on a giant hamster wheel going round and round and round until we learn what to do to stop it, but the only way to stop it is to find out what we can do to heal our souls because our souls—or our filters—affect the way we respond to traumatic events.

ALL REACTIONS TO STRESS ARE NOT EQUAL

Have you ever wondered why someone reacts to something that you aren't reacting to? Or why someone doesn't seem as upset as you are about something? There are several reasons why an incident is upsetting, or critical, to one person but not to another.

Our individual life experiences teach us so much about how to respond to stressful situations, whether we experience **eustress** or **distress**, but for now, we'll focus on distress. Growing up, we all experience a variety of difficult, painful, and stressful circumstances. As we face, manage, and walk through each event, we learn what helps us to feel better and what doesn't. We learn how to change our circumstances to fix the problem if we can, and we learn when we need to ask for help or if we can manage it on our own. Basically, we sink or swim.

As we face each new painful event, we repeat the same learning cycle, forming a new set of response patterns for each new type of event we experience. This ultimately becomes our unique coping style for that specific type of event. Some of these coping styles may be healthy, while others aren't. Some people may turn to drink, drugs, comfort eating, and other destructive coping mechanisms to numb the pain or avoid dealing with the issue. Others may find that exercise, talking to trusted friends and family, or prayer and meditation may help. Whatever we find that helps the first time, is generally what we'll automatically turn to the next time a similar kind of event happens. Whether you've chosen drugs, alcohol, or food, or the healthier options for dealing with painful events, if you believe they helped you to "cope" last time, any subsequent events of that type are likely to cause you to default to that same coping mechanism the next time. This response is purely because you've taught yourself that that's how you got through it before.

If you chose the healthier options and recovered well, it would be much easier for you to manage and overcome a subsequent traumatic event than someone who experiences that type of event for the first time. Your response would be less reactive than theirs because you've learned better coping skills for that type of trauma. You'd probably react to it more calmly because your mind has already got a programmed response for it filed away in your mental filing cabinet, so it isn't as terrifying now as it was the first time you walked through it. But for the other person who is experiencing it for the first time, they need your help to encourage and guide them through. That is one way they utilize an outside resource to recover, just as the city recovering from a disaster does. You are their outside resource. Along the same lines, if you and your family all survived a natural disaster such as a tornado or earthquake, your confidence that you'll survive the next one will naturally grow. But for someone who's lost loved ones in a tornado or earthquake, they're more likely to react negatively next time because their previous experience was one of loss and grief.

LEARNED SKILLS

Training is another example of something that influences how people respond to traumatic situations. For example, firefighters and police officers are trained for emergency response. Firefighters are trained to put out fires. They know exactly how to approach a house fire, what to do, what types of fire retardant are needed for each type of fire, and what breathing apparatus and equipment is needed before entering the house to rescue anyone inside. Police officers know how to handle a suspect of a crime, how to protect the crime scene, and how to protect the wider community if it's in danger. Doctors and nurses know how to stop severe bleeding, treat wounds, and save lives. In each of these examples, these careers have high levels of training so that each responder mentioned here knows exactly what to do in a crisis or emergency, especially when trying to save lives. Their training helps them not to panic. They've been so well trained that their confidence in their ability to handle the situation keeps them calm and focused.

What about you? What skills have you learned that you'd use in a critical event? Do you have some skills that could help you cope better than your neighbor and vice versa? I've been trained in law enforcement, the medical field, disaster relief, and trauma response, so I know how to calm someone down who's experiencing severe traumatic reactions, how to protect people, how to fight, how to dress a bleeding wound, how to do CPR, and what to do in major disasters. You may never have dealt with those types of things and may find them overwhelming or scary. My husband is an excellent contractor, so if anything breaks in my house, he can fix it. I am calm and confident because I know he is available with his perfect skill set to handle whatever comes up. However, when he's not home, and something breaks, it can stress me out because I don't know where to start to fix a broken appliance or plumbing leak. Can you see how some training can help someone to be calm and respond to a critical event more calmly than another?

BELIEFS

Different beliefs play a huge part. The word belief could refer to one's faith, or it could refer to one's moral code or accepted cultural practices. We're all very different, even if we're from the same town or country. For example, and this may be a silly one, but you'll get the point ... being from England, I believe that tea should be made with milk, not cream. Never use cream in tea! That is my belief, and it stems from my cultural heritage. Here in the U.S., however, many people think it's okay to use cream in tea! Joking aside, when it comes to disasters and tragedies, in western countries, it's very unusual and thus not okay for a child to die before their parents. In certain third world countries, however, where child mortality is so common, it's more readily accepted that children die before parents. So, when people of different cultures and faiths or moral beliefs face a similar traumatic event, their reactions will differ widely based on those principles which are unique to them. Is one better than another? No. Is one right or wrong? No. We're just all different, and that's okay.

When it comes to faith, I personally find that my faith in God strengthens me every day because I know He loves me, and no matter what I face, I know that He is always there to guide me through painful circumstances, which ultimately strengthens me along the way. He always has a way to make difficult things work out for good, and I can totally trust Him in that. I have done so for many years, and even though I don't like a lot of things I have to go through, He's always been faithful to show me (usually after the fact) why that was an important piece of my life's experiences and how it benefited me or others in my life. I can honestly say He's never been wrong. Others who have faith in a higher being apart from God may also find strength in their belief system. What's important here when dealing with someone's ability to cope with trauma, is to respect other people's expressions of faith or their lack of faith expression at all times. Their faith beliefs often influence their responses to stressful circumstances, and without that, they may not manage their grief or pain as well as they do.

One person's value in someone or something is different from someone else's. We all value different things to a higher or lesser degree than the next person. For example, if I crashed my car and wrote it off, it would upset me greatly because it's my car, my property, and I have to pay for it. That would be a huge loss to me, and I'd be understandably very upset by it. But it wouldn't upset you as much for my car to crash because you don't value it as much as I do. The same could be said if you lost a job, or a house, or a relationship that is treasured. It's only a highly stressful loss to you—meaning the loss is more critical to you because you place great value on what was lost. Your friends wouldn't necessarily react the same way because they may not value what you value to the same degree. That isn't cold or cruel, but your job loss does not impact them in

ALL LOSS IS NOT EQUAL. THE LEVEL OF TRAUMA EXPERIENCED BY A LOSS IS CONNECTED TO THE VALUE YOU PLACE ON THE THING YOU LOST.

the same way it impacts you, therefore, the level of stress caused by the event is lower for them. We see the same thing in disasters and traumatic situations. Those who lost something of great value, whether a material possession or a loss of a position, income, or loved one, are obviously going to react more than someone who lost very little or nothing at all. So, you'll always notice a huge range of emotions linked to the value of what a person loses. That reaction reflects how traumatic the event is to them.

PROXIMITY

Your closeness in proximity to a critical event (whether geographical or emotional), or to people or animals who've been impacted, makes a big difference too. When referring to disasters, it will certainly impact you more if the disaster happened in your home town and affected your friends and neighbors compared to it happening in a town in a different state where no one personal to you is affected. If it's out of your area and you hear about it on the news, you'd be concerned and maybe sad, but not necessarily traumatized, because it's not affecting any area of your personal life, or damaging any of your possessions. But, if that same disaster in the different state affected *your* loved ones because they were living there, then suddenly it becomes very personal. Let's take this a step further to look at it from a different perspective.

If you're a first responder, chaplain, or any other type of responder who's supporting people impacted by tragedy, there's a big difference between responding in your own town where you're familiar with the surroundings and people compared to being deployed out of your home town, state, or country. Yes, it's often more traumatic to respond in your own town because it's personal and too close to home. This is your community, your church, your schools, your hospitals, and shops, so, naturally, you'd want to protect it and serve it well. But, the plus side is that your familiarity is a great help because you know the layout of the streets, you know where to get supplies if they're available, food, water, and hopefully, you still have a home for shelter, so you find comfort in knowing your surroundings and having ready access to resources. However, if you're deployed out of town, your comfort levels may increase, and stress levels stay relatively low due to the fact that it's not so close to home, meaning you're emotionally more removed from the personal impact. Or, you could experience more negative stress and greater discomfort being out of town because when working in an unfamiliar environment, your stress levels can increase due to lack of sleep if it's in a different time zone, lack of familiarity of the area, not knowing where to get supplies from due to lack of local knowledge. Proximity plays a part in several ways, both positively and negatively.

STRESS RESPONSES ARE UNIQUE AND PERSONAL

Another example is if someone lives alone, without many friends, and their only companion is an old cat that means more to them than any human, they'd react with just as much shock and grief if their beloved cat died as someone who has lost their spouse would react. You cannot know the level of connection a person has to what they have lost, so it is important to be sensitive, not judgmental, to their reaction. So, can you see with each of these examples how everyone can experience the same event in a huge variety of ways that all create a huge variety of responses? All of them are considered normal responses to an abnormal event, and yet each response is unique to the individual experiencing it, based on all of these factors.

Self-care needs to be mentioned here too. We will go into this in more detail later in the book. Still, I need to bring it up here because it has been proven time and time again that healthy self-care habits that are already in place prior to a critical event make a lasting impact on how well a person can recover. Good self-care practices are vital to your overall well-being and play a huge role in stress management mentally, emotionally, physically, spiritually, and behaviorally.

Different factors, such as age, gender, race, disabled or able-bodied, fitness, health, good social support, or lack of support and faith, all have an impact in ways that I'm sure you can imagine and may have already seen or experienced.

My cancer diagnosis was a seriously critical issue to me, and at first, I went through the usual shock and trauma that I've already described. But I responded in other ways too, such as by bargaining with God, trying to protect some people, trying to stay positive and keep the atmosphere around me encouraging and trying to be brave while battling with my own pain and insecurities.

∾CB CR CB∾

My mind was plagued with intrusive images of Mum's traumatic death as the cancer ravaged her body and slowly squeezed out all life and breath from her in a most painful and ugly way. Those images and memories terrified me because I imagined that would be my experience, too, influencing the fear of my diagnosis. Confusion, shock, disbelief, and awful fear gripped me all at once. I was back on stage, reciting lines from that play about a woman called Fran who looked like me, talked like me, had a family and lifestyle like mine, but she was an imposter. Somehow, I'd been thrown into a parallel universe that mimicked mine, and I couldn't get back to the other side, the real side, MY side! I needed to fight to get back there. I needed answers, and I needed them now. I asked the hard question that I really didn't want to ask because I was afraid of the answer He might give me, but I wanted to trust Him no matter what the answer was. I really did.

"God, am I going to die? Is this cancer going to kill me?"

The gentle voice that I know to be His replied in my thoughts, "Are you willing to lay down your life for me?"

What? He must have misheard me. I was stunned. His reply shocked me; it scared me. That wasn't what I was expecting to hear. The boldness I felt a few moments earlier was obviously based on the assumption that He'd say, "No way, you're not going to die, silly! I am your Father, your healer, your provider, your protector. You are my precious daughter, and I'd never allow you to die that way."

I asked again in a different way. "Are you saying yes, I am going to die of this cancer that I have right now?"

Again, I sensed He was asking me, "Are you willing to lay down your life for me?"

It sounded as if He was actually challenging me to see if I was willing to die this way. I could feel my body go numb as if it wasn't already numb enough, and the awful feeling that just hits the pit of your stomach when you hear bad news. My mind raced through various death scenarios, trying to find the one I was most comfortable with before I answered. It was as if I could place an order for a specific final breath scene! I didn't understand His answer because it wasn't an answer. He answered my question with a question. I hate that!

I needed details, so I reworded the question, "Are you telling me that I am going to die within the next 6-12 months, or that I will get cancer again later in life and would die then? I know I'm going to die at some point, but now? With this disease? The way Mum died?"

His answer didn't change. It wasn't what I wanted to hear at all. How on earth was I going to reply to that? "NO! I don't want to die! I'm not ready to die yet. I'm only 49; I want to see my kids get married. I want to be a granny. I have way too much to live for, so no, I'm not willing to die, certainly not this way! But ... I know that 'no' isn't the right answer. I really don't want to go through this ... 'Lord, take this cup away from me! Nevertheless, thy will, not mine. My heart always longs to honor you and trust you, rely on you completely.'"

My brain was reciting those answers of obedience, but my heart was screaming the opposite. I needed to trust Him in all that He was asking of me. Was I really going to say no? A new level of boldness overcame me as a realization crept through my spirit that God was actually calling me to a season of such complete trust in Him that no matter what the outcome, He would be in total control and had a purpose, a plan that would be far bigger and more impactful than I could imagine. If He truly was asking me to lay down my life for Him, for His Glory, so that He could be made famous through my journey, then I wanted to be obedient enough to be used by Him. I knew that once I surrendered my life to Him, He'd give me the ability to walk it out. So, taking a stand, I began to pray with a strategy that would help me through. I asked God to do five things through me, for me, and for my family so that my cancer journey and death mattered.

I want to share these five things I asked God for with you now.

STRENGTH FOR OBEDIENCE AND FAITHFULNESS

"God, please give me the strength to be obedient and faithful to your call on what is left of my life, to the very end, no matter how hard it gets."

I truly did need His strength to do this. There was no way I could do this alone.

I had no idea what lay ahead. My experiential history with cancer was that all of my relatives that had cancer died of the disease, so I had no grid to encourage me otherwise. I was being put to the test. I had to surrender everything and trust Him.

GRACE TO FACE WHAT WAS AHEAD

"Please give me the grace to face the toughest days well, always representing you in such a way that no matter how hard this gets for me, everyone sees you being manifest in my life."

I desperately wanted my attitude, my faith, my words, and my expressions of God's faithfulness and love to be clearly seen by all who'd witness my journey. I needed His perspective and attitude flowing through me so that no matter what I endured, I represented Him well in every moment. I wanted to honor Him well and surrender all to Him totally. That is what I believed He was asking of me. To lay down my life in total surrender no matter what the cost. Even to death.

PROTECTION FOR MY CHILDREN

"Please protect my children's hearts. Let their faith in You remain strong, no matter what happens."

My faith had been shattered when Mum wasn't healed. I know many people lose faith in Jesus when they face disappointments and painful situations in life. They can get angry with God and turn from Him. I didn't want that for our sons and daughters-in-law. "Lord," I prayed, "protect them from false hope and broken dreams and keep their faith in you strong. Protect their hearts, minds, and spirits so that they still love you when I'm gone and help their faith in you to grow strong no matter what happens so that their hearts don't grow hardened or cold towards you in anger or disappointment or lacking in trust that you are always good."

WISDOM FOR MY HUSBAND

"Please give Rob strength and wisdom to know how to walk along this path. Protect his heart and bring him out the other side in total health and healing. Most of all, bless him with a new wife, one who'd love him far better than I do, so that he can find true love again, be happy, and not alone."

My heart broke for Rob. After watching my Dad face each day in fear, sadness, and intense grief as Mum neared death, I was so sad that Rob would endure the same pain. I longed for him to move forward from this with a healed heart. I desperately longed for him to feel deep love and to be loved again. I prayed for a woman that he'd marry. I prayed that he'd be loved as much as I loved him, and more. He deserved that. I longed for him to be happy and in love again.

GLORY FOR GOD

"Please make this final season of my life, and that of our family as we take this journey together, glorify You in such a way that we make You famous!"

I knew people would be watching us, caring for us, helping us, and praying for us. I longed for our family to use this time to glorify God by sharing His goodness, especially in the darkest times. I needed Him to help us all to be faithful, joyful, and happy, to the end, because of His goodness and faithfulness to us.

Telling our family and my Dad about my cancer was the hardest thing to do. Everyone took the news differently based on their age, life experiences, and personalities, but they all rallied round and did their best to be supportive. Due to the fact that Rob and I chose to be positive when we told them the news, it gave them the hope and confidence to believe for the best. Even so, we knew we still needed to allow each person to respond to this potentially life-threatening news in their own way, with the understanding that everyone always responds differently to bad news. We had to regroup as a family and trust that we would all rise again. ***RESURGAM.***

Endnote

1. Please see Luke 4:18-19.

TRAUMA AFFECTS EACH
OF US IN COMPLETELY
DIFFERENT WAYS.

FOUR

IT'S OKAY NOT TO BE OKAY

Did you know that it's okay to be sad? Angry? It's okay not to be okay—and sometimes it's out of your control anyway. We have been fearfully and wonderfully made. Our bodies are an intricate, miraculous network of precision and perfection, designed for a purpose. As much as ninety-five percent of all of our cognitive activity, which controls our decisions, emotions, actions, and behavior, takes place in our subconscious minds. This means that we only have conscious awareness or control of about five percent of our cognitive activity. Yet, the physical, mental, emotional, behavioral, and spiritual aspects of our design work in such perfect harmony that we do not need to pay attention to what's going on most of the time. Our bodies work 24/7, and our brains are constantly running in the background of our consciousness, monitoring all of our systems to make sure everything runs as it should. It's like the apps on our cell phones that keep running and updating in the background without our knowledge. We expect our phones always to work when we need them to, and we take them for granted until they slow down or crash.

We treat our bodies the same way. For the most part, we never pay any attention to how they function or what's going on in our brains, emotions, or souls. We just expect that they will do what they've been created to do day after day. When everything is running smoothly, we call it homeostasis, meaning that our bodies, minds, emotions, and behaviors are calm and peaceful, and we are in a homeostatic state of equilibrium. It's not until something goes wrong physically, such as when we're sick, or something changes in us emotionally, like when we feel sad after hearing bad news, that we notice the changes in us that feel uncomfortable or just "different." They make us take notice because we're aware of feeling negative stress, both physically and emotionally. Another example of just feeling a bit "different" could also be something as simple as experiencing some happy emotions that resemble positive stress after hearing good news, such as being told you're pregnant or that you've earned a promotion at work.

EUSTRESS IS THE GOOD, POSITIVE TYPE OF STRESS. DISTRESS IS THE BAD, NEGATIVE TYPE OF STRESS.

We often use the term "stress" to describe negative situations, but this leads many people to believe that all stress is bad for you, which is not true. Both **eustress**, the good, positive type of stress, and **distress**, the bad, negative type of stress, cause a stress response. Some stress is good for you.

64

EUSTRESS VS. DISTRESS

We all deal with various levels and types of stress every minute of every day. From the moment we wake each morning, we step into a world of time frames, busy schedules, over-booked calendars, deadlines, caring for family, sick relatives, planning meetings, or parties, preparing for the arrival of a new baby, a wedding, or packing for a holiday. Just having to think about what to cook for supper can be very distressful if you have no money for groceries. And yet, for some people, even if they have plenty of money for groceries, they can still be distressed about meals if they have to be creative about what to make for hungry kids who are fussy eaters. On the other hand, culinary creative people who love to cook could find these issues a positive and exciting challenge because it forces them to find creative ways to provide meals; therefore, they're feeling the eustress of the challenge.

In the first two examples, the stress response is a negative one because it's a *distress* response, but in the last example, the stress response is a positive one, so it's a *eustress* response. We are naturally designed to respond to various stressful stimuli, whether good or bad, positive or negative, in complex and simple ways.

Eustress (or positive stress) is good for you. It tends to motivate and energize you. It's often short-term stress because you have eustress when good, happy, and exciting things happen, such as buying a new home, having a promotion at work, or planning a wedding. Because it's positive stress, it's easier for you to manage it than it is for you to manage negative stress or distress. This is because eustress feels fun and exciting, so you tend to be energetic enough to rise to a higher level of performance in order to accomplish any goals associated with it. It also helps you to be more sociable. However, eustress can sometimes become overwhelming because you can have too much of a good thing, meaning that even though the stressful event is a positive one, managing that event can take so much out of you, or it can go on for so long that you're susceptible to being worn down by it, which can then lead to distress.

In contrast, distress has the opposite effect. It causes anxiety or concern and can have either short or long-lasting effects, depending on several aspects that I'll cover later. One of the main factors that makes something stressful to you is that it's usually outside of your normal range of experiences, which causes you not to understand how to deal with it. However, if you're repeatedly faced with the same negative issue day after day, you can learn how to manage it, how to overcome it, and deal with it in such a way that it becomes less stressful to you. It can become a normal part of your existence, and when that happens, there can be less of a stress response to the event because you've learned, over time, how to manage it. Having said that, things don't always work that way, and the ongoing stress can cause you to be overwhelmed to the point of causing you to be in a crisis.

STRESS RESPONSES TO CRITICAL EVENTS

When a critical event is outside of your normal range of experiences, it's outside your normal coping abilities. This leaves you feeling out of control, which causes unpleasant feelings of helplessness, fear, failure, and a host of other emotional responses that feel "yucky." The collateral effects of this are feelings of wanting to isolate yourself, withdraw socially, and lacking the drive or motivation to get things done. It's proven that the longer you're under acute stress, the more likely you are to have mental and physical problems such as depression, low immunity, and diseases.

In my line of work as an emotional first responder, there are several types of responses, or symptoms, that are commonly seen or that I'd expect to see, following certain types of negative, distressful events. There are also typical responses or symptoms I'd commonly see following positive stressful events. The most common stress responses I've seen are very normal ways of responding to changes that create exhausting and depleting demands on the mental, emotional, and physical coping skills of many of the clients with whom I have worked. In other words, we all have natural and common stress responses to abnormal events. Abnormal, meaning events that are out of our usual range of experiences. Such events cause stress responses that are typically seen in five main areas of life; physical, mental, emotional, behavioral, and spiritual. As we look at them more closely, you'll probably be familiar with some of the symptoms I'll talk about. Hopefully, it will encourage you to know that all of these responses are considered normal reactions to abnormal events, and your brain influences many of them.

PHYSICAL RESPONSES TO STRESS

If you're under so much stress every day that you're always feeling tired, foggy-brained, irritated, drinking too much coffee, and not eating properly, you will, over time, stress your body out more and more until you become ill. Your adrenals, the glands that release the hormones (adrenaline and cortisol) into your blood when you're in the fight or flight mode, work overtime. If you're constantly stressed, either due to chronic illness, or you have too many deadlines and unreasonable working conditions, or if you're in deep grief, which can go on for a long time, the fight or flight hormones continue to be pushed into your blood because that's a natural and autonomic defense response, meaning that it automatically happens subconsciously. These steps that your brain forces your body to take are all very common, defensive reactions for your protection, which are triggered as soon as your brain detects danger or detects that your homeostasis has been interrupted due to your stress levels increasing so much.

Have you noticed that your brain can't differentiate between a real threat or a perceived threat, so it often reacts to both in the same way? You could be watching someone getting violently attacked in a movie, or you could be watching it in real life. You're fully aware that it's not real in the movie, and yet your body reacts to both events in the same way. Both of those situations are dangerous because someone is physically hurt, whether real or pretend. Even though it's not you, nevertheless, your brain considers both examples to be threats, which interrupts your homeostasis. Those threats cause your brain to react defensively to keep you alive at all costs, so before you know it, your heart is racing, your pulse is beating, and your breathing rate increases. You clench your jaws and your fists, ready to fight. Your eyes dilate, and your whole body tenses up even if you're still sitting on your couch staring at the TV screen. It will stay in that defensive mode until the threat has passed. But your body isn't designed to constantly run at those high levels of stress for days and months on end, and it's not good for you to have such elevated levels of adrenaline and cortisol

> OUR BRAINS CAN'T DIFFERENTIATE BETWEEN A REAL THREAT AND A PERCEIVED THREAT, SO IT OFTEN REACTS TO BOTH IN THE SAME WAY.

for long periods. Your body needs to be able to relax, rest, and reset, which it can't do until those hormones wear off. They can be burned off as you fight or go for a long run and exercise at the gym. Or they'll slowly decrease and will be metabolized after several hours once your brain believes you're safe again.

Some physical symptoms are obvious when you're stressed, such as no appetite, headaches, unable to sleep, can't relax, and upset stomach, to name some of the basic more common responses. But those can worsen if the high-stress levels don't calm down or if they continue for too long. When that happens, we may notice more serious symptoms, such as dizziness, weakness, fainting, chest pains, grinding of teeth at night, increased blood pressure and heart rate, and nausea. So, to understand what your body is going through, you need to pay attention to all of the physical changes and the symptoms you notice when you're stressed. As you learn to pay attention, you will notice a familiar pattern of responses in your body. We're all unique and won't all respond the same way, but there are common symptoms we'd expect to see under acute stress. The more you pay attention to your body, the quicker you can recognize your own symptoms, which is your body telling you it's overwhelmed. But you must listen and pay attention to it because if you ignore it and keep pushing through, you run the risk of doing more harm than good.

Now please hear what I am not saying. I'm not saying that you should lie down every time you're stressed and take it easy or avoid the thing that is causing stress. You do sometimes have to pull up your bootstraps and push forward. Sometimes we just have to walk through dark days. Neither am I telling you that if you have a headache, your body is reacting to stress or every time you feel sick, you're stressed. You may have a headache because you didn't get to bed on time last night, and you may feel nauseated because you ate too much. So, please use wisdom when assessing your physical reactions to stressful situations. As you learn how your body reacts, you'll soon be in tune with it so well that you'll be able to manage your stress levels as soon you recognize the symptoms, rather than ignoring them.

BEHAVIORAL RESPONSES TO STRESS

Behaviorally, you may notice that you feel anti-social and want to withdraw. You may not want to see your usual friends or even some family members. Your appetite may change, so you eat more as a way of comfort, or you may eat less because your stomach is literally in knots. You may not be able to sit down and relax, so you pace and become irritated. Sometimes, highly stressful situations can cause us to lose our inhibitions, meaning that our normal moral compass can be affected in such a way that we make decisions that we'd not normally make when we're healthy, relaxed, and happy, resulting in making unwise choices. People under great stress have been known to have affairs, or alcohol or drug use may increase. Anything that will numb the pain will sound like a good option, but please avoid those at all costs. In the long run, these choices have huge ramifications and do more harm than good. All of these are common signs of acute stress. Be aware of them so that you can make wise choices and reach out for help rather than act out in unhealthy ways.

MENTAL RESPONSES TO STRESS

The brain is the most selfish organ in our entire body, and it has a phenomenal self-defense mechanism in it that causes it to protect itself and our body at all costs. It is the control room of every system in our body and controls everything our bodies do, both consciously and subconsciously. As mentioned earlier, ninety-five percent of our cognitive function takes place subconsciously, but it's all controlled by the brain. Everything from regulating our breathing to regulating our temperature, our digestion, sex drive, sleep patterns, fighting off diseases, and controlling our heartbeat. There's so much more that it does, of course, but for now, I just want to emphasize the point that those things are the things that we have no conscious control over. Therefore, our brain works constantly to keep us alive by ensuring that all of our internal systems work smoothly. If it senses any danger, such as a germ or virus entering our system, it goes on the defensive by releasing antibodies and white blood cells to fight the infection. The exact same thing happens to our brains when it senses stress. It goes on the defensive and instantly causes physiological changes to happen, causing us to go into fight or flight mode. Before we know it, we have adrenaline and cortisol pumping through our bodies to help us to survive the fight or help us to take flight to safety. This is another example of how stress can be good for you. It defends you.

> OUR BRAINS ARE DESIGNED TO TRIGGER THE RELEASE OF ADRENALINE AND CORTISOL TO HELP US SURVIVE THE FIGHT OR TAKE FLIGHT. THE STRESS RESPONSE IS THERE TO PROTECT YOU.

Some other mental or cognitive symptoms of acute stress or trauma are hyper-vigilance, confusion, nightmares and flashbacks, poor thinking and problem solving, difficulty remembering things, difficulty identifying people you know, poor memory, even an inability to remember things you know well, like certain words. When I was going through chemo, I literally couldn't remember words like hospital or hair salon! That's partly due to the stress of the illness, but also due to the medications I was on, which affected me mentally. So another aspect to be aware of is that medications can affect your brain function. If you're so overwhelmed that you've been prescribed some anxiety medications, they too will affect your emotions and cognitive ability.

ACCESS YOUR PERSONAL ASSISTANT

We can study the pros and cons of stress as we assess our behavioral responses in certain circumstances by looking at how our brains help us to process our stress levels before, during, and after each scenario. Imagine that you have a personal assistant, a mirror image of you only smaller, who we'll call Mini-Me, living in your brain. Mini-Me never sleeps and is sitting in the middle of a giant office filled with filing cabinets, some on the left and some on the right. On the left-hand side of the office, there are two different filing cabinets. Cabinet A is filled with empty files that have no labels on them because they're being kept for the times when you experience something you've never faced before. All of the files in the entire office started on the left in cabinet A. As soon as you face something new, a blank file from cabinet A is pulled out and labeled by Mini-Me, according to the event title. It's filed away in the second set of cabinets on the left, cabinet B, with the information about the event and your responses to it.

The files in cabinet B correspond to a variety of your experiences and keep track of each event, the ones that you're still responding to, or those that have passed but that you haven't found the right way to process to your satisfaction yet. Not because you're a failure in any way, but because you'd never faced that kind of event before, so you had no grid or reference for understanding or knowing what to do about it, how to react, think, or process it mentally or emotionally. You have no idea how it will affect you, what your needs are, and you could still be in shock, so you're not making the right decisions yet to aid your recovery. You're still learning how to respond to that event as you walk through it, figuring out by trial and error how to manage it emotionally and mentally while you heal.

Moving over to the office's right-hand side, you have thousands of cabinets all labeled cabinet C. Each cabinet on this side of the office is filled with files, clearly labeled, with a word that describes an event or experience that you have already faced in your past, and each file documents exactly what you did in each circumstance that helped you to overcome it or manage it in a positive and healthy way that taught you skills and responses that you will now automatically draw on in the future, showing that you have mastered each event well. There are so many more files on the right because as you've grown up, you've faced more and more of life's great experiences—tragic ones, hard ones, easy ones, happy ones, and everything in between. You've learned how to respond appropriately for your best interests, what works and what doesn't. So, as you've grown and adapted your responses over time, Mini-Me moves those files from cabinet B on the left to cabinet C on the right, when appropriate. You now have a huge amazing library of life, responses, learned behaviors, appropriate thought patterns, and choices in a variety of circumstances, some of which just become second nature to you. And all the while, Mini-Me monitors your responses and moves files accordingly. A lot of filing is done when you're sleeping, but we'll address that later.

When training a class or counseling others in trauma, I'll occasionally refer to this filing system because it's a great analogy to describe what occurs in the brain during some of our stress responses. When we are in total disbelief, or when we experience something so overwhelming that we go into shock, we may feel that we have a mental block and can't think straight or make any clear decisions about what we need, what to do, or how to respond. If someone is in shock, they can either shut down and become silent, almost frozen in fear, or they can become so overwhelmed that they literally can't move. That's because due to lack of training or prior experience, they do not have a learned behavioral response to that type of event. Mini-Me doesn't have a file for it yet. He's trying to quickly make one as you try to assess what the heck just happened or what you're going to do about what just happened.

TALK IT OUT

One way people process this is by talking. A lot. They begin to talk about what happened as a way to verbally process their pain, their disbelief, their anger, or grief, and they often repeat themselves over and over and over again. This is a very normal, and in fact, a healthy way to process strong emotions that overwhelm our usual coping systems. It is one of the behavioral responses called **cathartic ventilation**, and it's a very common response. The word catharsis means to clean out, cleanse, or purge. The word ventilation means

WHEN PEOPLE VENT AND TALK THROUGH A DIFFICULT EXPERIENCE THEY ARE TRYING TO PROCESS, THEIR STRESS LEVELS DECREASE AND THEY BEGIN TO FEEL BETTER.

to air out. So cathartic ventilation is the act of providing relief by venting or purging emotions and strong responses to stressful stimuli. As people vent and talk through the difficult experience they're trying to process; they begin to feel better. Their stress levels can begin to decrease, which is why "talking about it" usually helps.

Their minds are trying desperately to figure out where on earth this experience could possibly fit into their past experiences. They're trying to find answers to their cognitive responses, which are usually lots of questions, such as what the heck just happened? Why did it happen? How am I meant to respond to this? What can I do? Did it really happen? Sometimes people go into denial or disbelief, and it takes time for their brains to accept the critical incident as a reality. Talking helps.

As a person talks about the event—what happened, when it happened, how they feel about it, and so on—they hear their own words over and over again, which can help them to come out of the denial phase into the acceptance phase. Mini-Me makes a file for that event and puts it in the appropriate cabinet as they mentally and emotionally learn how to mitigate the pain, grief, stress, or trauma of what they've experienced. Then the next time their brain recognizes a similar event happening in their lives, they've already got some experience to know how to respond to it. Mini-Me removes the corresponding file from the filing cabinet on the right side of the office, cabinet C, and uses that prior experience to manage their stress responses to it again. This time, they can work through the stress faster because they've already been through it before, and they know what helps or what doesn't.

EMOTIONAL RESPONSES

Emotionally it's common to notice fear, anger, denial, panic, depression, and have outbursts or loss of emotional control such as intense sobbing or rage following something traumatic. Grief can be one of the strongest emotions. When your emotions are intense, you will usually feel overwhelmed because that's what makes the event that you've experienced so critical to you anyway. It overwhelms your usual coping systems. You're led by your emotions far more than you realize, so it's important to be in tune with them enough that you recognize their changes. When they become intense, it's because something has happened to change your mood. Pay attention to your mood changes at all times because it may help you to put a finger on the little things that agitate you. Awareness of what triggers you helps you learn to address your responses appropriately before things get out of hand. If you can practice this on a good day, you'll hopefully find it easier to manage them on a bad day. There's nothing wrong with allowing your intense emotions to flow freely if you're expressing pain or anger as a result of a traumatic experience as long as you're not hurting yourself or anyone else while doing it.

SPIRITUAL RESPONSES

Spiritual symptoms aren't usually mentioned in discussions of trauma. Still, I want to mention them here because this is another area in which I've noticed changes when I'm highly stressed or traumatized. Have you ever had a crisis of faith when going through a calamity? Or have you doubted that God cares or even exists? What about your ability to pray or listen to worship music or meditate on the scriptures? Sometimes if we're so upset that we let those aspects of our daily life slip after a critical event, we may struggle with guilt and shame because we separated ourselves from God in those dark days instead of drawing closer to Him. And yet, it's important to remember that He designed our bodies to react to acute stress a certain way, so He understands our pain and sorrow. It's okay if we feel the need to hide from Him for a little while if we're disappointed or angry. He still loves us unconditionally if we scream and yell at Him and ask why. Why me? Why now? God wants us to be real with Him at all times. He wants to hear us tell Him that we're mad, angry, tired, disappointed. He's got wide enough shoulders and can handle us being real and truthful with Him. In fact, He prefers that we are. It's when we're real with Him in that way that He can respond in His loving way to heal our hearts and show us the way through the darkness. We could feel hopeless and lack the faith that we'll pull through. I remember desperately praying for Mum when she was dying, convinced that God would heal her, but she died anyway. After that, I stopped praying for people to be healed if they were sick because I believed that my prayers didn't work in that area. That's a spiritual symptom of trauma.

⊸෴ ૭ଓ ૭ଓ ૭ଓ ෴⊸

Our history, our life experiences dictate how we will react or respond to the next similar situation. The important thing to understand is that we are all uniquely wired to respond to such events in certain ways that, at times, we just don't understand or even recognize. The fight, flight, or freeze reactions are natural stress responses over which we have no control. They happen within seconds, controlled by our sympathetic nervous systems. This is often followed by extreme ranges of emotion, such as uncontrollable sobbing to outbursts of anger, which can go on for days, weeks, and months. I learned to allow myself to express whatever I felt in that moment. If I needed to cry, then I'd cry. If I wanted to scream and punch my pillows, I did that. If I wanted to be quiet and solitary, it was okay. If I wanted to laugh out loud, that was fine. I didn't stop my emotions because I knew that wasn't going to help. **It's okay not to be okay.**

Our responses to highly stressful situations are normal reactions to abnormal events; however, they do change us in many ways. We often struggle and fight to get back to what life was like before the event. We want life to be normal again, but this is now our "new normal," and it takes some getting used to. It's not uncommon to grieve the loss of life as we once knew it or to grieve who we were before tragedy hit, and it brings changes in our bodies, minds, emotions, spirits, behaviors, and in our world that we may or may not like.

Strong emotions, especially fear, fueled my reaction toward the diagnosis of cancer in my body. My mind still held very vivid images of how awful it had been for Mum. I truly did believe she'd be healed of cancer because I fasted and prayed really hard! I had the whole scenario planned out in my mind and really did believe that my plan was so good that God would agree to it! Don't we all do that at one time or another? Yet we're shocked when He doesn't do things the way we imagine.

When I was diagnosed in December 2012, I had just returned home from a deployment with Foursquare Disaster Relief. I'd been working with a team of responders providing emotional and spiritual care to the survivors of Hurricane Sandy in Staten Island, New York. The stories I heard, the sights I saw, the smells I smelled, and the overwhelming experiences I faced were all incredibly sad. After working there for seven days, I was emotionally tired and overwhelmed with fatigue and stress. This was my first deployment with a disaster relief team, and I wasn't ready for what I saw and heard. I'd never witnessed such devastation or heard such tragic stories. Even my years as a police officer in England didn't prepare me for what I'd experience during that deployment. I was emotionally drained, shocked, and grieving for some of the people I met. Their stories were so tragic.

Storms can cause unspeakable damage. Hurricane Sandy was no exception. It totally changed the face of the east coast in many areas. Life is like that, though, isn't it? A storm crashes into our lives and totally changes us, how we perceive things, think, feel, react. As painful and traumatic as they can be, storms in our lives are sometimes survivable, and, with the right help and support, we do rise again from the floodwaters that try to drown us.

Because I received my diagnosis within a few days of returning from working with the Hurricane Sandy survivors, I was already vulnerable emotionally. That trip in itself was traumatic for me, and I hadn't fully recovered from it. I hadn't had time to process through all that I'd seen, heard, and experienced. So, I had two major traumatic events bowl me over simultaneously, compounding the trauma—creating the perfect storm to overwhelm my normal coping systems so much that my brain shut down. I'd never been through anything like this before and didn't know where or how to begin to work through my emotions. I struggled on various levels. Grief and trauma caused by the stories I heard, the scenes I saw, and the people I met who touched my heart so deeply on my recent deployment, mixed with the fear and grief that came with cancer, believing I was going to die the same gruesome way Mum did. I was not okay.

SHORT-TERM VS. LONG-TERM DISTRESS

Another aspect to be aware of is the difference between short-term and long-term distress. Short term stress can be caused by a single event, whether it's eustress or distress, and easily manageable. It is short-term because either the stressful event passes quickly or it's an event that you've experienced before, so you've already learned how to respond to it. This is especially helpful if it's a negative type of stress because you are prepared to face it in such a way that it allows you to mitigate its effect on you. In other words, you've built some resilience and resistance to it, so your confidence has grown, which empowers you to adapt your response by learning a coping technique that enables you to regain some control in the situation. This then helps you to manage the situation well, which in turn decreases your stress response.

Long-term or ongoing stressful events (such as terminal illness, ongoing financial struggles, various forms of abuse) tend to be more serious and continue for extended periods. These difficult long-term events are harder to manage and recover from. This is compounded when you don't know how to react to something due to it being out of the usual range of your personal life's experiences or expertise. Certainly, as time goes on, you can learn coping skills that can help manage stress, but it takes longer to find your feet and figure out how to regain control of your situation or manage the stress reactions you experience. However, as with short term distress, over time, you can learn to adjust and adapt to the difficulties you're facing and gradually manage them in such a way that could potentially help you to recover over time. It's okay not to be okay. Whatever you are walking through right now, you will rise again from the ashes of your despair and painful circumstances. ***RESURGAM!***

FIVE

WHAT'S HAPPENING TO ME?

By now, you know that during and after a serious traumatic event, our brain triggers several reactions all at once, immediately. It's so fast that we can feel physical changes almost before we know what's hit us.

In this excerpt from my blog that follows, you'll notice several symptoms that we typically see in someone experiencing trauma, and you'll notice how Rob and I responded differently to the same situation. I often wondered what was happening to me because I felt as if I was going crazy, but now I know that both of our reactions were normal.

ᕯ ᏨᏜᏨᏜ ᕯ

My days were very confusing. One minute you're traveling through life without too much trouble, then suddenly something crashes into your once 'normal' and happy world, commanding you to change everything immediately. This season of 'new normal' life came with a mad rush of appointments, consultations, blood work, more biopsies, prods, and pokes that caused more pain and severe bruising in my arms and right breast. During this time, I had several phone calls with a dear friend, Mick, a pathologist. I needed his help and advice. With all of the decisions that had suddenly been thrown at me to make, I knew he'd steer me in the right direction. Decisions such as which surgeon to see, who would be the best oncologist, and where to have my treatments.

Mick was such a gift. He took it upon himself to make several phone calls for me, arrange my appointments with the best surgeon, oncologist, and medical team in town. More importantly, he kindly offered to oversee all my pathology throughout the course of treatments personally. He knew who to call and who'd give me the best care. I was blown away. I didn't have to lift a finger to sort anything out. Within about an hour, he'd made the necessary arrangements for my next few days, which meant that all I had to do was just turn up for my appointments. Even from the start, God was already intervening, already paving the way showing me where to place each step in this journey. He'd placed Mick in my life to care for me in this way. That was so incredibly encouraging. Naturally, I was overwhelmed and very stressed; I couldn't even think straight. Thankfully I didn't have to. My mind shut down as if mentally blind again. I needed someone else to show me the way because I was too overwhelmed to know where to start. I desperately needed an outside resource, and Mick was it. He was a lifeline for me throughout the journey in so many ways and on many occasions.

The first "port" of call, so to speak, was a surgical consultation to insert a port in my chest. Chemotherapy is known to weaken and injure smaller veins, such as those in arms and hands, so Mick said that having a port in the main artery in my chest was a better way to go. It meant that all of my blood work and my infusions would go straight through the port and protect my veins. Less pain, less hassle, and less damage. Less stress!

Next, Rob and I went to see the oncologist for our first consultation with Dr. D. It had only been a week and a day since we were happily driving to the fun party with friends in San Francisco when that dreaded phone call came—how life had suddenly changed. Dr. D. was such a friendly, amicable, and kind man. He started explaining a few things about the type of cancer I had, the pathology results, the necessary treatments, the drugs I'd need, the frequency, strengths, how many rounds of chemo, blah, blah, blah... It was too much. I couldn't take it all in.

My brain was numb and struggled with information overload. I tried to take notes but couldn't even figure out how to write down everything he was saying. My ears heard what he said, but it didn't stick. When I tried to remember what he'd said, I'd miss the next point he was making. Rob was strong for me. He went into his male brain 'logical' mode and was in control, protective, and seemed at peace with this new adventure. I am so glad he was with me in that office because I couldn't remember much of the conversation. I was a nervous wreck whose brain had totally shut down due to the stress of this traumatic experience. I was still in shock and felt as if the bubble that swallowed me up when I was first diagnosed was still surrounding me and keeping me locked away from my old life.

Dr. D. was very patient with me as I kept asking him to repeat himself just so that I could understand what the next two weeks would look like. I needed to break it down into smaller chunks of information to digest it all. When someone is in shock and trauma, they really can't take in what you're saying to them. They try to. But their brains just turn off, like mine did.

The tears started rolling down my cheeks as the overwhelming fears and emotions became too much. I apologized for crying and told him that I knew I was going to die, like Mum, but I didn't want to die that way. The conversation I'd had with God when He'd asked me to lay down my life for Him was firmly stuck in my head, so what was the point of all of this treatment? Why prolong the inevitable? Yet a flicker of hope was inside me, screaming at me to fight back and 'do' something about it. We were with him for one and a half hours, and I really can't remember much of what he told us. But one thing I do remember him saying, with a slight giggle in his voice in response to my comments about dying was "Die? You're not going to die of this cancer."

What? More shock, an about-turn, a "wait a minute" moment followed by a desperately begging glare, which I'm sure shot straight from my eyes right into his. I was stunned. I'd been on the brink of emotional death, drowning in the waves of negative beliefs and terrifying images of Mum's gruesome battle. Confused, genuinely believing I was slowly dying, suddenly, this stranger who'd been thrown into the deepest, most intimate area of my life without warning was throwing me a lifeline! Did I hear him correctly? I asked him to explain, which he did, assuring me that while this breast cancer is indeed one of the more aggressive types, it's also one that's been more thoroughly researched. Therefore, there are some very effective drugs available to fight it. He went on to say that it was easily treatable, and we'd caught it so early that I had a very good prognosis. Because I was young, fit, and healthy, I should sail through chemotherapy without any issues.

Now I couldn't wait to start my treatments, knowing the longer I went without them, the higher the chance cancer would spread throughout my body and grow in other areas where it might not be found until it was too late. I was still filled with fear, afraid that it was creeping through my veins, in the dark where I couldn't see it. It was lurking in hidden places only to jump back out at me later in life, mockingly planning my demise. It was like being taken over, slowly, by an alien that I couldn't see, didn't understand, and couldn't control. I so desperately wanted the chemo to start so I could kill the cancer before it killed me.

⇜ ଓ ଓ ଓ ⇝

You may not understand what your brain does in emergencies, but you need to trust that it's beautifully designed for your protection and that it will make your body naturally do things to handle the stress you're in. This is normal. It's important that you have some understanding of how your brain and body react in acutely stressful situations. You'll find that with an increased understanding of these reactions, you'll recognize them when you next experience them, and rather than those feelings causing you alarm, you'll appreciate their purpose. This will help you feel better about what your body is going through. You won't be asking yourself, "What is happening to me?"

The parasympathetic nervous system controls homeostasis and the body at rest. It is responsible for the body's "rest and digest" function. The sympathetic nervous system controls the body's responses to a real or perceived threat and is responsible for the "fight, flight or freeze" response. The parasympathetic and sympathetic nervous systems are part of the Autonomic Nervous System responsible for the human body's involuntary, subconscious functions. This accounts for 95% of the cognitive activity that we've already mentioned. The sympathetic nervous system responsible for the fight, flight or freeze response causes hormones—adrenaline and cortisol—to be dumped into your bloodstream when it senses danger.

WHEN IT SENSES DANGER, THE SYMPATHETIC NERVOUS SYSTEM RESPONSIBLE FOR THE FIGHT, FLIGHT OR FREEZE RESPONSE DUMPS ADRENALIN AND CORTISOL INTO YOUR BLOODSTREAM.

I know we've already talked about them, but I want to explain more about how they help you in stressful situations. Each one causes different involuntary reactions to protect you. No doubt, you've already felt the rush of adrenaline when you get frightened, such as when you have to slam on your brakes to prevent a car crash or when someone jumps out at you to startle you. Adrenaline increases your heart rate so that it pumps your blood throughout your body faster, increasing blood flow to your brain and muscles. It also makes your body release more sugar for instant fuel, which is turned into energy. It constricts your blood vessels in your arms and legs to move the blood to the inner organs as a form of protection for them and also so that if you're injured peripherally, you won't lose much blood. It also dilates your air passages to increase your oxygen intake, which keeps your breathing more efficient.

Cortisol gives you bursts of energy to keep running or fighting; it lowers your sensitivity to pain so that if you're injured, you can keep fighting. It also increases your memory function. Have you ever been in a traumatic situation where you suddenly seemed to remember something you learned in school or college many years before? Something that you've not thought of for a very long time and didn't even know you knew? Yet that memory is exactly what you need to know in order to handle the emergency at hand. You suddenly have focus and can make decisions based on what you didn't remember knowing. I heard a story of a man who took a CPR and First Aid class some 15 years before his neighbor collapsed due to a heart attack. The man hadn't thought of his CPR training in all that time and had never used it since becoming certified. Yet, at that moment, his mind suddenly remembered all that he'd learned about CPR, enabling him to save his neighbor's life. That is increased memory function. Sometimes, especially under the influence of an adrenaline dump, different things will be going on mentally and emotionally, and you run the risk of freezing. The freeze response is another involuntary, self-protection response which is controlled by your brain. If your brain perceives a threat that it doesn't have an appropriate response for, it may decide that the best protection for you is to freeze until the threat passes. No matter how good your coping skills are, you may be so overwhelmed that you may not respond as you'd like to. Please don't allow yourself to feel guilty or ashamed that you didn't do this or should have done that. This is something that you can't control and there's nothing you can do about it.

You've probably heard people talking about being "triggered." This is a great example of how your body jumps in to fight or flight mode before you can even say the words "hot potato." You may be triggered when something reminds you of a very painful event or experience in your life, and suddenly those same stress reactions and feelings that you experienced when you were really going through those hard days erupt in your body without warning. For example, when a soldier is being attacked by the enemy with bombs, guns, and other missiles, his brain immediately sends signals to various parts of his body for survival. His adrenal glands release high amounts of adrenaline and cortisol to prepare his body for battle, the fight or flight mode, and for self-preservation at all costs. His brain constantly assesses danger signs and what his body needs to keep fighting and to stay alive. It sends alerts through the various neurological systems to heighten his awareness, focus, energy, speed, strength, blood, and oxygen.

It happens in a millisecond. In this state, when he's fighting for his life and the lives of his comrades, the sounds of explosions and guns signify death, destruction, and total annihilation. He's been so traumatized by the sounds of explosions around him in battle that when he's walking through town one day, several years later, and hears a car back-firing, it triggers a reaction. For most of us, we wouldn't react because we'd recognize the sound for what it was and ignore it. But when the soldier hears it, it retraumatizes him because his brain learned and remembers that those sounds meant severe danger and death. The sound of the car back-firing could cause his body to involuntarily react as if he were still in the heat of battle. His trauma response, or trigger, would be to hit the deck or run for cover in less time than it would take him to think through what to do. His brain instantly goes through the same process of going into fight or flight mode to protect and stay alive, just as if the soldier was still in battle. This causes the same fears, panics, and physical reactions as before, only beginning to calm down after a few moments once the soldier realizes that the threat isn't real.

My mother loved to play classical music. I'd hear her classical collections floating around the house emanating from her office as she worked at her desk. Since she died, every now and then, if I hear one of her favorite pieces of music when I'm in a mall or driving, without warning, I can be reduced to tears. Anything can trigger you at any time. The other day, I was looking for something in my office. I opened my desk drawer. I pulled everything out to try to find it, and at the back of the drawer, I found an old purple velvet bible cover that Mum had embroidered as a child. As I held it, time stood still, and I had a flashback of seeing it in her office when I was young. I was suddenly aware of how much I missed her, and it brought a lump to my throat. Flashbacks can be caused by triggers too.

Triggers aren't always sad or negative. They can bring back happy and fun memories, such as the smell of your favorite cookies reminding you of baking with your Mum or Granny when you were a child, or the smell of wood chips reminding you of working with your Dad or Grandpa in their woodshop. It's so soothing when wonderful memories come flooding back to your mind. But the term 'trigger' is usually used in a negative sense.

Your previous experiences, the interpretation of those experiences, and your memories of them cause your brain to send you an urgent message to let you know that what's happening is dangerous and potentially life-threatening or safe and harmless. Always remember that whether good or bad, your previous experience will usually dictate your response to repeated similar events. Use this knowledge to make careful choices about your life. Protect yourself, if necessary, by choosing not to go to places that may bring up bad triggers but only avoid them until you've healed enough to cope with your stress reactions to those unpleasant places.

It's important to work towards healing rather than allowing the negative emotions to keep you trapped or keep you from living a full life because you can't go to certain places for fear of being triggered. Choose safe places that will bring good memories too, places that bring calmness and peace. If necessary, until you're strong enough to handle some negative reactions from unhealthy and toxic relationships in your life, choose relationships that encourage you, fulfill you, not ones that cause you to feel unsafe or to feel fear or anxiety. Give yourself permission to make those choices for yourself. Put clear boundaries around what you will and won't do, where you will or won't go, or movies you'll see, or with whom you will or won't be in a relationship. Stick to your guns until you feel safe enough to move your boundary lines in your own timing and not because someone else puts pressure on you to do so or makes you feel stupid or guilty for having boundaries in the first place.

This is your life. You are responsible for your own emotional and mental health. No one else can make these choices for you. Others may advise or encourage you to make choices that they believe are good for you, but unless you feel completely safe with them and know that they truly do have your best interests at heart, and you trust them, have enough courage to speak up and be bold and firm about what feels right to you. It is okay to say, "no." That way, instead of always having to ask yourself, "What's happening to me?" as I did when I experienced stress reactions or triggers, you'll understand what triggers you and makes your stress levels rise and why it's happening. Believe that you can rise again. **RESURGAM**.

SIX

LINES IN THE SAND

Think of your house where you live now and imagine a big yard around it. A lovely spacious yard that's protected by a tall, sturdy fence. The fence can be designed in any way you like but picture the fence going all around the yard and house so that the entire yard and house are securely protected inside the fence line. There are only two gates in the fence; one gate is for cars to come and go, and there's a smaller gate just for people. This fence is the legal boundary line of the property that you own and have full authority over. You decided how and when to put the fence up and exactly where it would sit on the property so that you could clearly establish the boundary line around your property. Even if you're renting your current home rather than owning it, you legally have authority over it and are responsible for it. Everything that is within the fence line of this property is yours. Everything outside the fence line belongs to someone else.

You have the freedom to leave and enter your yard by using the gate to walk through the fence at any time of the day or night, and you never have to ask permission from anyone else. It's your yard. Your fence. Your gate. You own it. You care for it. Your friends and neighbors do not have the right to enter your yard at any time unless you give them that right. You can do that in two ways. You can choose to permit them to enter if they phone ahead of time to ask if they can come to see you. You have the choice at that moment to say yes or no. The other way they can enter your property is if you instigate a visit by inviting them first. In each example, you are the one deciding to grant them permission to come on to the property via the gate. It is never their decision. In both of these examples, if you allow your visitors to come in, they'll stay for a while because you wanted to spend time with each other, which was the main point of the visit.

What if someone wanted to come into your yard to retrieve a ball that bounced over the boundary fence line between their yard and yours? That would just be a quick visit, in and out to grab the ball. They don't even need to come to your doorstep. They'd stay in the yard area but only briefly. They certainly don't have permission to play in it, or set up their patio furniture in it and have a bunch of friends over for a BBQ, or put up a tent and stay there without your say so. If they did come in without your permission, they'd be trespassing. They'd be ignoring and abusing the physical boundary—the fence line—that establishes the privacy of your yard.

Like the mailman or a UPS driver, delivery people have 'implied permission' to cross your boundary line into your yard. Implied permission means that due to the fact that you've ordered something or have mail coming to you, it's implied that they have permission to deliver the items to your door. There's an assumption, which is okayed by you, that they may enter your yard and knock on your door to bring you something that you're expecting, such as mail or a package that you've ordered on Amazon. Our pest control guy has implied permission to enter our yard to treat our property for unwanted pests once a quarter. He already has permission to enter our yard because we've paid for his services and have agreed to terms with him to provide those services to us. He can enter at a prearranged time, do his job, then leave, but he only has access to our yard and garden shed. Never our house. If I found him in my house at any time, he'd be trespassing, and I'd probably call the police immediately.

So, now that we've discussed the outer boundary of the yard, let's consider your actual house. It follows the same principle but takes it a step further, to a deeper level, an inner boundary. Some people may be welcomed into your yard, but not your house. Your house is reserved for very special people: friends and family, those that you know well, people you trust and have healthy relationships with. These friends have proven that they respect you, your boundaries, and are careful to treat you and your home and your yard in such a way that won't cause damage. Some friends may only enter your house when you invite them in. Others that you're more intimate with have permission just to knock and walk in. Family members, especially those living in the house with you, or maybe a roommate, don't need to knock first. They can just walk in because they've been given that right to do so. Depending on who it is that wants to enter your yard or your home, you will naturally put them into a specific "boundary category" based on your relationship with them, which is based on how well you know them, together with mutual trust, love, safety, and respect.

Can you see where I'm going with this yet? The fence line I described is a very clear boundary. It's even a legal boundary, and I described it this way so that I could use this analogy to reference you, your life, and your personal boundaries. You are the house and yard, they represent the totality of your life, and the fence is the boundary you establish around your life. A personal boundary is a defining line that separates individuals from one another. It's like drawing a line in the sand to establish the no-go areas. There are areas in life within your outer boundary line that belong only to you, and there are areas in life outside your boundary line that belong to someone else. Everyone has an invisible boundary that they are allowed to put around their life, around the things they have authority over and the things for which they are responsible.

> A PERSONAL BOUNDARY IS A DEFINING LINE THAT SEPARATES INDIVIDUALS FROM ONE ANOTHER.

The word authority means to have the power or right to give orders, make decisions, rule over, and compel obedience. This concept can be applied to all aspects of our lives, not just physical space and time. Your body, your thoughts, your relationships, your beliefs, and so many other things that belong to you should have personal boundaries set around them. Anything you have authority over requires an intentional boundary to be placed around it. In fact, life can be a mess unless you put up personal boundaries. Without having healthy boundaries in place, you could be harmed by forceful people who are eager to control areas of your life that they have no right to control. Without boundaries, you're also more likely to be exposed to and succumb to temptations that could have been easily avoided.

Boundaries serve as a way to communicate our comfort level and what our individual limits are. Healthy, strong boundaries help us to feel safe and secure. They give us confidence, empowerment, and self-control. They're very important for every stage of life and help to shape our identity. A personal line in the sand around you is also the defining line that separates your identity from others. It also defines what you have authority over and what you don't. It is vital to understand this when it comes to establishing healthy boundaries around body, mind, emotions, beliefs, and feelings.

There are definitely some negative effects of having boundaries broken by others or of not having healthy boundaries established in the first place. Broken or no boundaries could result in you having toxic, abusive, controlling relationships rather than healthy, trustworthy, safe ones. Boundaries are not just physical such as "Don't get too close to me." Boundaries are also emotional such as, "I refuse to allow myself to be upset by you." Boundaries are also spiritual or mental such as, "You can't tell me how to think or what to say or believe."

When learning how and when to set boundaries, a helpful question to keep in mind is, "Is this situation helpful to me, safe for me, or ultimately supporting my recovery?" If not, you need to set a boundary. Boundaries aren't just a sign of healthy relationships; they're also a sign of self-respect. So, give yourself permission to set boundaries and work to preserve them. But what does all this have to do with trauma? A lot! Following is a blog entry about how boundaries helped me find a safe place and safe people along my journey.

❧ ℭ℘℘ℭ℘ ❧

As soon as word began to get out about my diagnosis, all of a sudden, people thought that they were experts on the subject. So many people wanted to tell me about their own personal experiences with cancer or tell me about Uncle Joe's sister-in-law's cousin's son's battle with the disease. I really didn't care about anyone else's story or advice. I just wanted to be left alone to figure things out for myself. People tried to get me on special raw diets or juicing or eating more broccoli, and some even told me just to rely on the healing power of Jesus, as if I didn't know that already! The information was overwhelming, and it was making me angry. I knew in my heart that all of these pieces of unsolicited advice were generally offered in love and with all good intentions, but people were really beginning to get on my nerves with it all. It was overwhelming me. If I wanted advice, I'd have asked for it, and when I did ask for it, I went to very select people that I invited and gave permission to speak into my life. Not every Tom, Dick, and Harry that thought they knew me well enough to start telling me what I should do!

Slowly but surely, I began to shrink back into an emotional corner. It was a self-protective reaction to unwanted advice and comments, not to mention the countless questions thrown at me. Such as how are you feeling? Are you alright? Is there anything I can do to help? I felt as if I wanted to scream at people to go away and leave me alone. I was screaming inside, but I was smiling sweetly and thanking everyone for their concern on the outside. I was too afraid of offending them or hurting their feelings to really tell them to leave me alone. The last thing I wanted was another suggestion from anyone! Instead, I dealt with it by avoiding people. I stayed home more. I avoided places where I'd bump into someone I knew, just so I wouldn't have to talk to anyone and answer more questions or even talk about the Big C. I didn't even want to go to church (which actually surprised me); church didn't feel like a 'safe' place for me at that moment. Everyone knew me. Too many wanted to chat and ask me how I was doing. I couldn't get from my car to my chair without being bombarded with questions and comments. Now, in reality, it may not have been that bad, but that's how I felt. I couldn't slip into church quietly, pray, worship, or enjoy the service because I felt that everyone was looking at me, watching me. I'd avoid eye contact just so people wouldn't start a conversation. I'd sit and cry, sometimes hiding behind my sunglasses because I didn't want people to see the tears. That would just invoke more people trying to comfort me and talk to me. All I wanted to do was just be left alone, to pour out my heart to Jesus without feeling watched or smothered! I started going to church late and made my escape before the service ended, just to avoid the conversations. Then, I stopped going altogether while I went through the rest of my treatments. I felt guilty about it at first but soon realized that again, this was a normal reaction to a traumatic and overwhelming event. In other words, if we're already in a very difficult season of life, and our normal routines cause extra stress, such as going to public places when we don't have the desire or capacity to talk to lots of people, it is okay for us to go into a self-protective mode. As long as someone, or a few intimate, trusted people have access to us to make sure we don't totally crash and burn or isolate for too long, it's okay to pull back and have privacy when we need it. It is good for us because it gives us the breathing space we need to process what's going on, what we need in each moment, and it gives us permission to figure out the answers to those questions in our own way and in our own time. Too often, well-meaning people have been known to crush others and do more damage by saying things like "you should be over this by now" or "you should be doing this, that, and the other."

I have learned from my personal experiences that when I am having a seriously hard time with something in my life, I want to be left alone to figure it out with Rob, with my immediate family, and of course, with Jesus. Only very few people, my close inner circle of friends, are allowed into my intimate space. You know the people I mean? Those friends that you can call at any time of night or day and they don't mind. Those friends that would lovingly and happily take you to the hospital and sit with you for hours until you were either discharged or visiting hours were over for the day; those friends who you don't mind seeing you naked when you need a bath or shower while your hubby's at work and you haven't got the energy to climb in or out of the shower or bathtub because you're so weak, let alone dry yourself; those friends who sit with you and hold your hand, cry with you, pray for you while you're going through chemo and your hair is beginning to fall out.

During this journey, I learned to find my voice. I learned that it's perfectly acceptable, even healthy, to put up boundaries around you. It's healthier for you and kinder to those trying to help you if you establish early on the parameters within which you feel safe and secure. I gradually learned that even though most people asked how I was, because they genuinely did care, I was still within my rights to refuse to talk to them about myself, the cancer, and the horrid journey if I didn't want to. I soon grew confident in being able to gently and kindly say to people, "Thank you for asking, but right now, I don't want to talk about it." I found that when I did that, I felt more empowered to be able to face the crowds and side-step the hard conversations that I'd been avoiding by just letting people politely know that I was not going to talk to them about the cancer unless I felt able to in that moment, or ready to, or even wanting to. Some days were easier than others, and each time I decided to put up a boundary or to answer people's questions, it was always determined by how I felt in the moment, who they were, and whether or not I wanted them to know my business. I learned to give myself permission to have the conversations I wanted to have with whom I wanted to have them. In that season of my life, I allowed myself to understand that I could put my needs first for a change and choose my interactions and conversations based purely on those needs. That was liberating!

I LEARNED TO GIVE MYSELF PERMISSION TO HAVE THE CONVERSATIONS I WANTED TO HAVE WITH WHOM I WANTED TO HAVE THEM.

Another way to put a safety boundary around you to avoid answering all of those well-meaning questions and conversations is to have a spokesperson. I decided early on that if anyone outside of my 'inner circle' wanted to know anything or offer any help, they could not speak to me directly. They were all encouraged to speak to Rob, or my three closest friends who supported me the most at that time, Susan, Felisa, or Dawn. No one else. It helped to protect me from countless phone calls, emails, and texts. Please don't misunderstand me here. I was amazed by the amount of love and concern that *people shared with me, and I really did appreciate it. Unless you've been in a situation where you're so overwhelmed with stress and fatigue that you can't cope with the extra effort it takes to reply to everyone, you won't understand. I literally had no capacity to manage social interaction. I had no energy mentally or emotionally to engage with everyone that tried to engage with me. So, as a step of self-preservation to save my energy for allowing my body to rest and fight the sickness, I had to put up healthy boundaries around parts of my life that needed protection. I needed to delegate some of my responsibilities to others for a season. It is okay to do this, and I'd encourage you to allow yourself to do the same if necessary.*

❧ ✿ ✿ ✿ ❧

One of the first steps on your journey to healing from trauma is establishing a sense of safety. Remove yourself from people who overstep your comfort zones in any way, boundary busters in your life, people who don't respect your needs and personal safety. Know your limits. Find your voice and clearly state what you will and won't allow, what you do, and don't feel comfortable with, and believe that it is your right to establish healthy boundaries around every area of your life that needs one. You'll soon learn who will respect your boundaries and who won't. You can then adjust your relationships accordingly and remember that you are never responsible for other people's reactions towards your boundaries. If they don't like your boundaries and don't respect them, it's usually because you've taken away their control over you. But it's not about them; it's about you. Yes, you're right; this is easier said than done, especially if you've never understood boundaries or if you've never been allowed to have them. But just start small by establishing some safety nets around you, and your confidence will soon grow in this area. Be bold. Be strong. Believe in yourself, and know that it's always okay to say no! In fact, by saying no to something, you're saying yes to something else, and you can control that part of your life. If you say no to attending a party tonight that you have no interest in going to, you're saying yes to yourself. You are saying yes to spending your evening in any way you choose, which frees up your time, mind, emotions, and choices to do what you want to do that evening instead. That is drawing a line in the sand and putting a boundary around your free time to spend it as you wish and with whom you wish. If you're asked to volunteer your time for a good cause again and again, to the point where you're overly tired, over-committed, and don't have the time to do other things in your life that need to be done, it's okay to pull back or step away completely. Your time is your responsibility, and it's within your boundary of authority to dictate how to use it. Say yes to the things that are a priority in your life by saying no to the voluntary commitment that drains you.

Some very important benefits of healthy boundaries are self-respect, value, and worth. Good boundaries help create healthy habits that bring peace, strength, assertiveness, confidence, and self-control. They also help with mental, physical, spiritual, and emotional health, joy, and empowerment. They establish safe, healthy relationships and give you your voice back so that you're confident about not sharing what you don't want to when you don't want to. You'll learn only to share when you feel safe and only share as much or as little as you choose, and to whom you choose. Trauma can make you shrink back, which is normal, so these boundaries will help you feel protected in your most vulnerable state.

A word about self-compassion: the most important boundary you can set is to become aware of the judgments and blame you place on yourself. Most traumas you experience are not your fault, and recovery from them will take time. Allow yourself the grace and compassion needed to help you grow and gradually rebuild safety in your relationship with yourself and others. You are worth it.

I also want to mention your responses to other people's boundaries. How do you normally respond to someone who's found their voice and draws a line in the sand? Do you find it easy to respect their boundary, or do you find that you push through it to get what you want? The truth is that we all do that at times. It's normal behavior to push other people's boundaries from time to time, but that doesn't make it right. Please respect their boundaries as long as their boundaries are reasonable. For example, an elderly or infirm person is putting up a boundary that dictates they don't want any help in their home because they fear losing their independence. But if you know they need the help to keep them safe, then those boundaries have to be pushed a bit for their good. This could enable them to live independently for longer rather than being in an assisted living home. Other than that kind of situation, don't be a boundary buster.

If someone you know is putting up a boundary, there's a very good reason for it. They either feel unsafe, unprotected, or maybe they just need space for a while. It is okay to ask them about their boundaries. It helps you understand their needs and respect them and gain wisdom about that person's current situation and concerns. By respecting them, you show that you care for them and that you're supportive of their decision to find their voice and make personal choices over their own lives, which is their right to do. We all need that type of friend in our lives. Maybe you could even help people that you know to recognize their need for boundaries and encourage them to establish some if you see areas where they might help. Boundaries bring protection around you in your most vulnerable areas. They provide time and space when you need to heal, especially from trauma, which helps you to rise again. *RESURGAM.*

IT'S OKAY TO ASK OTHERS
ABOUT THEIR BOUNDARIES.
IT HELPS YOU UNDERSTAND
THEIR NEEDS, RESPECT THEM,
AND GAIN WISDOM REGARDING
THEIR CURRENT SITUATION.

SEVEN

YOUR DEFENSIVE STRATEGIES

The word "defense" refers to an act of resisting attack, defending you from harm. Is it possible to have a defensive strategy against acute stress and trauma? Yes, it is, but it's not going to stop bad things from happening to you. Neither is it going to turn you into a superhero who'll never get injured or distracted when in a fight. It just adjusts how you'll respond to those painful and stressful events that affect us all, mentally, emotionally, physically, spiritually, and behaviorally.

Self-care is your defensive strategy. We hear the term self-care a lot these days, but it wasn't prevalent in our vocabulary 20 years ago. What does it mean? More specifically, what does it mean to you or me? Self-care refers to the choices we should make and the practices we can regularly incorporate into our lives that help us stay as healthy as possible in the five main areas mentioned previously.

SELF-CARE REFERS TO THE CHOICES WE SHOULD MAKE AND THE PRACTICES WE CAN REGULARLY INCORPORATE INTO OUR LIVES TO HELP US STAY AS HEALTHY AS POSSIBLE MENTALLY, EMOTIONALLY, PHYSICALLY, SPIRITUALLY AND BEHAVIORALLY.

Part of self-care is education. We have to study, ask questions and learn what to look out for when we're feeling overwhelmed with life's challenges, whether they're normal everyday things or more critical things that knock us off our feet. Looking at the five main areas more closely, I'll explain why it's important to know what to look for so that you can integrate some excellent self-care practices into your life. This is especially helpful before a critical event happens. Let me explain how you can create a positive self-care defensive strategy, a plan of preventative action, tailor-made to suit your needs so that you can rise again after being knocked down by life's hard lessons.

It's important to understand that self-care doesn't start when something terrible happens. It starts today. For self-care to be the defensive strategy that it's meant to be, you must get comfortable with personal self-assessments in several areas of your life and then adjust your habits and choices as necessary when you notice something is off-kilter. Start now. The best and kindest thing you can do for yourself today is to begin assessing some elements of your lifestyle choices that either help or hinder your recovery from slight inconvenient stressors to major traumas. To be effective in personal care intervention, especially during acutely stressful circumstances, you must begin by establishing healthy habits of good boundaries and good lifelong defense habits, which means taking care of yourself before, during, and after stressful and traumatic events and creating healthy habits that become automatic to you. So automatic that your healthy choices come naturally, rather than you having to figure out what to do during a serious crisis and then battle against your will to do the right thing. That's stressful enough!

PHYSICAL SYMPTOMS

Let's start with physical symptoms. It's a known fact that many of our sicknesses and diseases are, in fact, stress-related. If more people understood how their bodies reacted to stress or the unhealthy things done to them, either through neglect, ignorance, or if they've been hurt by someone else, I believe they'd be more likely to defend their physical well-being by caring for their bodies in such a way that they'd be stronger and healthier, resulting in fewer medical issues. To be defensive physically means taking care of your body in such a way that protects it.

These defensive habits begin with preventive maintenance, which means maintaining your body, mind, and emotions in a state of homeostasis and healthy balance. Most of these things you've heard so often that you're probably bored of hearing them but trust me, they do work and are important to your overall well-being; such as reducing refined sugars, caffeine, unhealthy fats, and excess salt and cholesterol. These may be self-explanatory, but for those asking themselves why those things should be avoided, I'll briefly share my thoughts on how eliminating them will help your body feel better and be healthier, allowing it to cope with the effects of acute stress much better. If well cared for by you, the added benefit is your body not succumbing to so much sickness, aches, pains, inflammation, and many other symptoms.

For our bodies to manage the myriad of things we put them through, it's important to be educated about what we can do to keep our bodies healthy and able to fight off the negative side effects of stress and bad habits. For example, refined sugars are known to cause insulin resistance, diabetes, obesity, and create a higher risk of cancer because cancer feeds on sugars. It goes without saying that unhealthy fats cause obesity, heart disease, stroke, and other issues, such as increasing the bad cholesterol, LDL. LDL can cause a build-up of cholesterol in your arteries, whereas healthy plant-based fats increase the good cholesterol, HDL, which carries cholesterol to your liver to be flushed out of your body. If your arteries are clogged with cholesterol, and you have a sudden adrenaline rush, which causes an increased heart rate following a scare or a shocking trauma, imagine what happens to your heart and body when the blood can't flow through your clogged arteries smoothly. That's a heart attack waiting to happen. If you're obese and have to run away from danger, you won't get very far at all before you're fatigued, sore, and unable to run anymore. I'd highly suggest buying organic foods and grass-fed meats if at all possible. I can hear you all now telling me that those foods are too expensive and you're on a tight budget. I understand your frustration, and I used to argue that point myself. I learned to change my view on that when fighting cancer. Diseases stress your body out. The more stressed your body is, the weaker it becomes. Your immune system is then affected, causing you to be more susceptible to other ailments and physical symptoms. When you're sick, the usual response is to treat you with medications made with chemicals that have other negative side effects. They may treat your first symptoms but can cause others. It's a horrid cycle, and it needs to be broken.

My story is a classic example. Obviously, I had chemo to deal with cancer, but I was absolutely shocked at how quickly chemo destroyed my body, from head to toe. Literally, within just a few short weeks, I rapidly changed from being an energetic woman who enjoyed the gym, being on my feet at work all day and never getting tired, walking my dogs every night and never getting breathless, to my body feeling so heavy and weak that my legs couldn't support me to walk from the bed to the loo. I couldn't walk a quarter of a mile without regular breaks where I'd literally have to sit down to rest. Then walk a few steps before sitting again. I lost all of my hair, nails, and had neuropathy in my hands and feet, as well as other ailments that I had to endure while on chemo. Here's a blog post I wrote at the time that describes the journey. You'll see that despite the trauma I was going through, my sense of humor stayed intact. It was one of the few things I could rely on that kept me going.

⋘ ൦ ൦ ൦ ⋙

Gagging on food and drink that tastes like stagnant pond water was not something I ever thought I'd be doing. Whoever thought of force-feeding oneself on nutrition that tastes that bad? It literally does make me gag. Nevertheless, it has to be done. My taste buds have been destroyed after just one treatment, although only temporarily, I'm told—jeez, give me a break! To me, the enjoyment of food is the taste and smell, but when those senses are missing, there's no enjoyment in eating. That's why I hardly eat anything, but my oncologist says I must keep eating because my body needs the energy to keep fighting the disease, plus to keep healing the damage the chemo is doing to the healthy parts of me. It's become a tasteless, unenjoyable chore that is keeping me alive.

What's so odd is that I've lost my senses of taste and smell, but my sense of pain in my mouth is on high alert. I can't eat anything too warm or that has pepper or spice added, no matter how mild it is, because my mouth is so incredibly sensitive and sore that it feels as if I've put boiling water into it each time I have any food in those categories. Chemo damages the skin in many ways and chronically dries out moisture from many areas of the body, and my mouth is one of those areas. The very thin, dried-out skin in my mouth has broken out in little sores on my tongue, gums, and inside my cheeks. Added to that, I battle with a tongue that feels as if it's been shaved raw with a dull razor – those are all side effects of chemo – it's intensely painful all the time. I have a strong mouth wash that I use before eating anything. It numbs my mouth so that I can eat without pain. I can't even enjoy my cream sherry anymore because alcohol burns my mouth and throat. Not that I could taste it anyway right now, but it's one of the pleasures in life that I enjoyed.

Fingers and toes. Who needs them? They're overrated! Right? Wrong! My goodness. I have neuropathy in my extremities. My fingers and toes are numb. Dead. Do you know how hard it is to do up a button, a zip, to hold a knife and fork? And you can forget about chopsticks! It's even hard to hold a pen and write when your fingers are numb. I feel like a two-year-old who needs help dressing in the mornings because I literally do, depending on what I'm wearing that day. My toes are tingly and don't always feel the ground I'm walking on, so it can feel as if I'm not touching the ground. That will mess with your head, let me tell you!

With numbness in my hands and feet, taste buds that can't taste, a nose that can't smell, and a stomach that reacts violently to the medicines I'm given to counter the chemo effects (that's an oxymoron) by causing chronic diarrhea, a painfully dry mouth AND a bald head that makes me look like an Observer from the recent Fringe series on TV, I have to see the funny side of life. It's not all so bad!

So, let's focus on the positive. I've discovered that being bald is quite liberating in a way. This is a good time to save some pennies on shampoo, hair appointments, razors, and shaving cream. Actually, I don't use shaving cream, but you get the point. I now save time in the mornings because I don't have hair to style. This is cool! I just throw on a hat or scarf if I feel like it and get on with my day. I also don't have to spend money on razors for a few months and have the smoothest legs and armpits that I've had in years! Haha! My eyebrows and eyelashes are still clinging on for dear life but are losing that battle hair by hair!

This really can be a positive experience and a great time to learn more about a minimalist lifestyle. But who am I kidding?? This is a tough journey, and I'm just the type of person who tries to find the humor in things to make the experience easier. I reflect on life and think to myself ... AT LEAST I'M STILL BREATHING!

Seriously though, this can be funny. It's all a matter of perspective. This would be a great time for me to lose a little weight. I have some spare padding 'round my middle. No one recognizes me anymore without my long thick locks! I went out for a walk today and waved at people who I know really well as they drove past me ... they didn't respond. It was as if I was invisible. They seriously didn't see me, or maybe they just thought I was some nutter trying to be friendly, so they ignored me. Let the fun begin ... I can now travel about in 'stealth mode' and get up to mischief without getting caught.

⤙ ଓ ଔ ଓ ⤙

Chemo is poison! There are no two ways about it. I know it kills cancer, but it also kills healthy cells too. My entire body was poisoned for five months while I was on my regular treatments, but chemo drugs stay in your system for a long time after the treatments end, so the poisoning continues. Can you now understand why, after seeing what happens when my body is given such toxic chemicals, that I decided I'd rather spend my money on more expensive, non-GMO, organic, healthy foods? I fed and fueled my body properly, giving it the best advantage possible with the high quality, nutrient-rich foods to help it to rebuild and repair itself. Poor quality, nutrition-stripped foods that are covered with chemicals were poisoning my body even more. I'd rather invest my money in the best quality, clean foods to keep me healthier and more protected, rather than not caring for myself properly and paying even more money on medical bills and prescriptions because I hadn't taken the necessary defensive steps to protect my body from some of the preventable physical issues when I could.

OUR SKIN

Another aspect here is that our skin is the largest organ in our entire body. Did you know that skin is an organ? Well, it is. It's through your skin that many toxins are absorbed. So, as well as being careful with what you put inside your body, please also carefully assess what you put on your skin. Remember, a defensive strategy is assessing your life in various ways. This is a great one! Assess the products you use on your body and change them if you can, yes, men and women. Use high quality, clean-living, organic body butters and facial creams, makeup, and shampoos and hair products, deodorants, which all help defend your body from toxins that weaken it slowly and poison you.

STAY HYDRATED

Cut out excess caffeine, sodas, and alcohol. Those drinks can dehydrate you—especially those laced with caffeine because caffeine is a diuretic. Good hydration is just as important as a good diet. Drink plenty of water. One reason staying well hydrated is vital is because your brain is made up of mostly water, about seventy-five percent, so it needs plenty of it to stay healthy and perform well. We've already looked at how important your brain is to your survival, so keep it healthy and keep it hydrated, or it will not be able to function as it should.

Being dehydrated can cause your brain to become foggy and perform poorly. One way to know that you're hydrating properly is to check your urine. It should be clear for the highest hydration rates, or at least pale yellow. Now I know that some vitamin supplements can discolor your urine, but my point of telling you about the color is part of the education I mentioned that's so important. It is important to have a quick way to check that you're drinking enough, and the color of your urine is the quickest and most reliable way.

HARMFUL SUBSTANCES

Smoking, drugs, excess alcohol use, and other substances also negatively affect your body, as we all know, so I won't go into as much detail with those, but you get my point. They're not a good habit to have and certainly aren't helping your defensive strategy. They're more offensive to your body, and they automatically deplete your physical ability to be as healthy as you can be. Therefore, your body's ability to respond well to stressful situations starts off at a deficit.

HABITUAL USE OF HARMFUL SUBSTANCES INHIBIT YOUR BODY'S ABILITY TO RESPOND WELL TO STRESSFUL SITUATIONS.

When I refer to drugs here, I'm not just talking about the common interpretation of drug abuse that many of you may assume I'm referring to, such as amphetamines, cocaine, or heroin, plus other illegal ones. I also include the abuse of prescription drugs. Many people who're faced with unbearable emotional and physical pain may abuse prescription medications for all sorts of reasons, so it's worth mentioning it now because that's obviously not a form of drug abuse that's often thought of. These are common ways people use to numb the pain of grief or deal with their emotional reactions to trauma, but while it's understandable to want to dull the pain and escape the nightmare of traumatic responses, these are not the way to do it. Any substance abuse is likely to cause way more damage to your physical body than the emotional trauma does. Healthy defensive habits, such as the ones I'm sharing in this chapter and throughout the book, can help you find other coping mechanisms to deal with the pain you're experiencing.

TAKE CARE OF YOUR BODY

It's important to understand that if you expect your body to run from danger, fight for your life, or manage the increased stress it will experience when you go through traumas, you must make sure you keep it in excellent shape. You probably don't appreciate exactly how much energy is used up when you're facing trauma. Your brain causes your body to go into overdrive in so many ways, burning up energy as it keeps you safe. Just the mental and emotional stress can be exhausting. Have you ever been through a stressful day when you've really done nothing more than sit at your desk or on the couch, and yet by the end of the day, you're so tired that you have to go to bed early or take a nap during the afternoon? That's because your body uses up so much of your normal energy levels trying to keep you safe, kicking your internal systems into overdrive. Even though you can't see it and don't understand what's going on, you can feel the pep in your step fade. So, other than the things we've discussed, what else should you do to ensure that you can sustain high energy levels in a crisis?

Exercise! Yes, that old chestnut! The more exercise you do after a traumatic event, the quicker the cortisol and adrenaline are burned up, meaning that those hormones that keep you in the fight or flight mode won't stay in your system for as long. That helps your heart rate slow down again, and you'll find yourself feeling more restful sooner than if you sat on a couch. Now I'm not saying go out for a five-mile run following a traumatic experience or go to the gym and lift weights for an hour. Sometimes going out for a brisk walk is all that is needed, depending on the person's physical ability, but at least do something and build up from there. Start small and increase as you're able to. But if there's any doubt about your ability to exercise, please see your doctor first so that they can confirm that you're able to do this.

Exercise also burns off increased stress, helping you to be more relaxed. It helps your brain to be less foggy, so you're more focused. Good exercise also helps to oxygenate your body. The more oxygen you can get to your brain, heart, lungs, and muscles, the better you feel and the more energy you have. It's a healthy habit circle that helps you thrive because more energy gives you the desire to be more active. The more you exercise, the stronger your body gets. The fitter and stronger your body becomes, the more you're able to do because your energy levels increase. Overall, the healthier and stronger your body is physically, the more protected it will be from negative physical side effects of acute stress, and the easier it will recover from an emotionally traumatic event. If you don't stop making bad choices and start caring for your body in the ways I've mentioned above, it may become ill, weak, and unprotected and will eventually just stop working. My slogan is that if you don't stop, your body will stop for you.

REST AND SLEEP

This is equally as important in the area of rest. If you don't rest when you need to, your body will eventually stop for you because it will crash. Sleep and rest are vital. We've all heard the advice that we should get at least eight hours of sleep a night, and for me, that is certainly true, but it's a general guideline, not a hard and fast rule. The reality is that not everyone actually needs that much sleep, but some people need more. Some people manage well with seven hours, and others need nine, but it's not just about the length of sleep, the quality of sleep is also very important. Most of us equate good sleep to having great energy. You probably already know how much sleep you need to help you feel your best physically and whether you need to have a break in the day for a nap. But what about your brain. Does that need sleep? Let's look at some sleeping facts that you may not have known so that you understand why sleep is so important.

After just one sleepless night or even a very late night followed by an early start that cuts your usual sleep time down to between three to five hours, your brain begins to lose its ability to function properly. You feel foggy, sleepy, and may struggle to focus. We can all cope with at least one or two nights like that over Christmas, New Years', or on other special occasions. Still, if you continue to have interrupted sleep or just not enough sleep, your brain will soon only be able to function at about fifty percent of its normal ability. Yes, just half of its usual power and capacity to manage all of the things it's expected to manage on your behalf every minute of every day.

We've chatted about the brain a lot already—the importance of its ability to keep you safe, and how it operates continuously in the background like your phone apps do, always monitoring things to make sure your body stays alive and healthy. But if that main organ isn't getting what it needs to continue to do its job, you are at risk of a myriad of issues. Not only mentally but emotionally and physically too. Lack of sleep steals your capacity to cope with things that you'd normally manage easily. Emotionally you can get irritated and moody. Mentally your brain goes foggy, and you lose focus. Physically, a tired body has a depleted immune system and is open to more aches, pains, and ultimately, diseases.

Sleep is vital for your brain, and I'd even venture to say that it's more important for your brain than your body. Without going into too much detail in this book, let's scratch the surface of the correlation between your brain and sleep by looking at the sleep patterns and why they're so important for you. You have several sleep cycles throughout the night, and I'm sure you've heard of REM sleep and deep sleep. REM is the abbreviation for rapid eye movement, and during the REM cycle, you have a lot of brain activity, almost as if you're awake, which is when you tend to dream, and your eyes dart back and forth a lot. Then we have deep sleep cycles. Do you remember the analogy I gave of Mini-Me working in the office in your brain constantly filing away all of your experiences? Well, a lot of that happens while you're in a deep sleep. That's when your brain heals, regenerates itself, and processes the events of the day, organizing your memories, your stressful situations, and your joys into its files for long-term storage.

During deep sleep, your body also releases important hormones vital to restoring and healing wounds, repairing damaged cells, and helping your body grow and develop. This is why, when you're sick, it's so important to rest. When you're in trauma, it's just as important to rest—your body actually does need you to rest more so than usual during those times because it has to work overtime to heal the damage that you've experienced, whether emotionally or physically. So, deep sleep, as you can see, is critical to your healing and just as important when things are going well for you because the healthier your body and brain is, and the more rested they are, the better you'll be able to cope with the stresses of life. If you're stressed, overwhelmed, or exhausted in the middle of the day and can't lie down to rest, there are other things you can do which will help enormously, such as deep breathing, meditation, prayer, and other relaxation techniques.

AVOID TRIGGERS

Do you remember when we talked about triggers and how they can affect you? Well, one defensive strategy is to permit yourself to avoid them until you're confident that they won't retraumatize you. It is okay to say no to doing something, or to going somewhere, or even seeing someone if you know it might trigger you. It's okay to give yourself permission to use your boundaries to protect yourself from being retraumatized. To do that, you need to be acutely in tune with your personal history of traumatic events and difficult personal experiences. When you recognize situations that could pull you into events similar to traumatic events from your past, or if by engaging in something that would cause more pain or a trigger response, then stop! Assess the situation and decide whether or not your involvement in that event or activity, or engaging with that person, is going to hurt you or not. Be kind to yourself, please, and permit yourself to make the right and necessary self-care choice for you.

> IT'S OKAY TO GIVE YOURSELF PERMISSION TO USE YOUR BOUNDARIES TO PROTECT YOURSELF FROM BEING RETRAUMATIZED.

This is especially true if you're in a caring profession such as a first responder, pastor, doctor, nurse, therapist, or chaplain. As you'll remember, some trauma is caused by building distressing events upon events which compound until finally there's one event, usually not even that serious, which puts you over the tipping point and breaks the camel's back. I appreciate that if you're employed in a caring profession, it's not as easy as it is for a volunteer to pull back from duty due to emotional and mental health needs and stress responses. However, now that these mental and emotional health issues are more readily talked about and taken seriously in several career fields, it's getting easier to be more mindful of our own needs and get help when needed.

This doesn't mean you should avoid helping others in times of need. It means that you should be aware that doing so may affect you. You either avoid that situation by finding someone else to help those in need or choose to help anyway, knowing that you need to be extra vigilant to monitor your own stress responses afterward.

LEARN WHEN TO SAY NO

Many people in caring careers, especially volunteers, tend to overcommit themselves and aren't always good at saying no. Please let me encourage you to say no when you need to. That is a great self-care habit. I work with people in emotional distress and trauma weekly. Sometimes daily. There are times when, due to the horrid stories I hear and the vast amounts of energy I use up just listening to countless tales of trauma, death, grief, and everything in-between, plus the things I see when I'm deployed, my mind, my body, soul, spirit, all get wounded. They're all affected by the job I do, and that comes with the territory of being an emotional trauma responder, disaster responder, and chaplain. But, I've done this long enough to know my limits and also to know what self-care habits I need to use in certain circumstances to keep me balanced and healthy.

At times, when I'm overtired or struggling with grief and emotional pain due to my work, I know I need a break to rest and regroup, and restore my soul. During those times, it's not unusual for me to get a call about another suicide or a call to deploy yet again to lead a disaster relief team for about a week to ten days, and I just know that I've hit a brick wall, so I say no. I won't go, and I am totally okay with that. I didn't use to be at the beginning of my career, but I've learned the importance of pacing myself. If I were to agree to go, I'd be harming myself because I've run out of energy, emotionally and physically. I have nothing left to give; I'm totally empty. In those moments, I decline to go; I put myself and my needs first and stay home. I'll go and soak in my hot tub, have a massage, or go and stay for a few days in a remote cozy cabin with my husband to regroup, rest and recharge. That is being mindful of my self-care needs.

I also look ahead on my calendar and block out dates and weekends from time to time to make sure that nothing is booked on those days. I'm usually booked out at least 6-8 weeks in advance, so I need to do that; otherwise, I get so busy that I never have a break. Emergencies don't come on a schedule and don't run on a 9-5 shift either. So, I have to block out a whole week or two weekends in a row, in advance, just for breathing space. That's a great habit to get into now before it's too late and you become overcommitted. Once you're overcommitted, if something happens to overwhelm and distress you, your coping systems are too exhausted to carry you through that season well.

Try to keep at least one weekend every month free of any commitments, and if you find extra free time on your calendar from someone canceling an appointment or a meeting, please don't fill it! Give yourself extra time to just 'be.' If you're married, if at all possible,

> ONCE YOU'RE OVERCOMMITTED, IF SOMETHING HAPPENS TO OVERWHELM OR DISTRESS YOU, YOUR COPING SYSTEMS ARE TOO EXHAUSTED TO CARRY YOU THROUGH THAT SEASON WELL.

try to get away with your spouse for a private weekend at least once every 4-6 months. You can never, ever invest too much in your marriage or your mental health; trust me, I'm speaking from experience. My marriage and my emotional and mental health are doing well because I take that time to put those important habits on my calendar.

HEALTHY RELATIONSHIPS HELP YOU COPE

Maintaining healthy relationships with friends and family and associates at work are also important healthy and defensive habits because we're designed to be in a relationship, not isolated, lonely, and separated from social circles. If our relationships around us are happy, fulfilling, and bring us joy, we feel connected, loved, welcomed into society, and also have a great support system around us when things go wrong. I'm not intimating that all relationships have to be happy all of the time; that's not being realistic and normal families aren't like that—families fight, friends have misunderstandings— that is being human. But I'm saying that overall, if you have good relationships with a wide circle of people, you will be healthier in the long run because your social network is part of your survival net.

It's been scientifically proven that people in relationships and those with good social circles tend to live longer, more fulfilled lives than those who don't. Think of times when you've been distressed or in grief, and think about how you reacted. Did you want or need someone close to you to be with you and support you? Yes, of course, you did! That's because we've been wired to need connectivity with others—especially during hard times. Now, there are also times when you're grieving or traumatized that you need to be alone and have healthy boundaries (as I explained when I learned of my cancer), and that is fine too, but being alone and isolated is best in short time frames, it should never be long term.

SPIRITUAL HEALTH

Your spiritual health is just as important as the other aspects of health we've looked at in various ways. Whatever "spiritual" health means to you is fine. It's your journey, so you're free to interpret that as you wish, and understandably, not everyone who reads this book will necessarily believe what I believe or who I believe in. But, we should each find a way to express our spiritual beliefs and faith and draw on them for strength and encouragement as we journey through trauma or acute distress. I'll share what that looks like to me as I practice my faith when it comes to keeping myself spiritually healthy.

MUSIC

I enjoy listening to music, many types, such as praise and worship music, classical music, jazz music, any music that helps me to keep my mind focused on our amazing creator, God. Music that lifts my mood and brings me joy. Sometimes it's slow and gentle and helps me to relax, settle down, and rest. Other times it's upbeat and rocky and keeps me motivated to keep going when the going gets tough. Music is a great mood enhancer. I enjoy meditating on the Bible and using its teachings to help me understand how to live life, make choices, and help others. I pray and ask for wisdom, emotional strength, peace, understanding, and knowledge of how to face each situation.

AVOID THE MESSIAH COMPLEX/ SAVIOR SYNDROME

I do my best to still my voice and outside distractions so that my heart can sense the right way to go and so that I can make sure I don't rush into situations in which I'm not meant to be. Just because I do what I do does not mean that I'm responsible for responding to every call for help. Others are equally, if not more qualified than I am, so I pay attention to whether or not I'm to respond, and the Lord lets me know when I ask Him.

It's all too easy for those of us with caring hearts and compassion to want to drop everything and run every time the alarm goes off, but the reality is that we are not meant to respond to everything. Some calls are for me and others aren't, and only God knows which is which, hence the need to listen carefully. If I don't listen and allow myself to totally trust that He knows exactly which responder would be the best for that person in need, I run the risk of stepping into areas of false responsibility. As soon as I step into that area of false responsibility by thinking that I can fix a situation or by believing that I'm the only one qualified to help, I'm stepping into pride and arrogance and taking on a burden that was never mine to take.

Let me put it this way as I describe something that I've both seen and experienced time and time again. God loves everyone way more than you, or I could. He sees all things. He knows what each of us need every day. Therefore, it goes without saying that if someone is in trouble, He can pick the best of the bunch to help that person. He cares that much. He chooses which responder would be the perfect fit and which responder will have the best approach, experience, and personality to handle the job. So, if the alarm goes off and I'm asked to help, I stop, take time to breathe slowly, and assess the situation before making my decision. Sometimes I just know that I know that I know I'm to respond.

Other times I can sense I'm not meant to, and that is where many people find it hard to put the brakes on. Those of us who are chaplains or those who work as emotional and mental health responders tend to run towards the tragedy rather than away. We can often believe the lie that if we don't respond, that person won't make it through this crisis without us. There are times when that may be true, but only God knows which times those are, so stop and listen to His nudge telling you to go. If I feel at total peace about going, I go. If I have any reservations or sense that it's not right to go, I don't. But I will often ask someone to go in my place and then leave it in God's hands, knowing that He is in total control and ultimately responsible for all outcomes. This is one huge way in which my spiritual well-being is kept healthy. I never assume I can do it all, nor do I expect this of myself. I just listen and follow His lead. If I have responded, I always make sure I spend time afterward with Jesus assessing how things went, how my heart is doing. If necessary, I speak to another chaplain or a counselor if praying and worshiping with plenty of rest, fresh air, exercise, a healthy diet, good hydration, and social support isn't helping.

OUR BEHAVIOR IS AN INDICATOR OF OUR OVERALL HEALTH AND WELL-BEING

Our behavior is largely governed by our moods, mental well-being, emotional peace, and physical health. Would you agree that our behavior tends to be better if all of those areas are doing well than if one or more of those areas is off-kilter? It goes without saying that to keep our behavioral responses to life's difficulties under control, our souls and filters have to be as clean and healthy as possible.

Our behavior is usually a learned response to how we perceive a situation, whether good or bad, and our behavior manifests as it runs through our filter first. It happens so fast and automatically that we often behave without thinking, and then sometimes we regret our behavioral choices.

Remember the vacuum cleaner filter? You want to make sure that your soul and your filters are clean so that your dirt doesn't get pushed out into the air via your behavior. None of us are perfect, so we won't get this right every time, but I do want you to be aware of this aspect of health and wellness because we do have a choice here. If we're not doing well and we're irritable or sad, we must learn to slow our thinking down enough to assess whether or not a behavior pattern will be beneficial or harmful to us and those around us. That is what you're doing when you put it through a filter. You are choosing to leave your dirt behind and let fresh air come out into the world.

You can now see why being as healthy as you can possibly be is so important before, during, and after a traumatic event crashes into your life. You have to constantly assess every area of your life and think about which strategic habits you should be using now. You seriously won't be able to cope well if you're not as healthy in all of these areas as possible. I've only scratched the surface of how your mental, emotional, physical behavior and spiritual health can help you cope with such painful times.

YOU WON'T BE ABLE TO COPE WELL WITH STRESS IF YOU ARE NOT FORTIFIED IN YOUR MENTAL, EMOTIONAL, PHYSICAL, AND SPIRITUAL HEALTH.

EDUCATE YOURSELF

There is one last thing you must do. Keep educating yourself. Because education is all about gaining information—and information brings hope! The more information you have about these things, the more hope you'll have in your heart, and you'll be better able to ride the waves of trauma. You'll know what to do. You'll have learned more about what is or isn't helpful, resulting in more confidence that you'll be able to rise again from the acute stress or the depths of despair. Also, you'll stand up tall and strong and pay it forward as I'm doing right now, ready to share what you've learned with the next person. Nothing goes to waste!

Please remember that you, and you alone, are fully responsible for your health and well-being in all of these areas. Only you can make the necessary choices you need to make, such as what to do, when and how to do it, to remain able to cope with all that life throws at you as best as you can under the circumstances. You need to have the self-respect and determination to do what is right for you. I'm not saying it's always going to be easy. I'm certainly not saying that by incorporating these healthy habits into your life today, you won't get the wind knocked out of you tomorrow. I am saying that you'll be able to pick yourself up, dust yourself off, and pick up the pieces of your life easier than you would have if you hadn't established these habits.

HUMOR AND A HEART OF GRATITUDE

In addition, having a good sense of humor and a heart of gratitude are great defensive strategies against many things, so let me encourage you to laugh a lot more and be grateful for your many blessings! Laughter and joy lift up our spirits and emotions. It helps us to feel better about the hard times we're facing. Even in the midst of deepest despair, it's possible to crack a joke, think of someone else worse off than you are, and find a silver lining around your cloud. My oncologist told me that I did so well during my cancer journey, despite the awful aspects of it, because I always tried to be positive and grateful. I'd find the silver lining and was often cracking jokes and just trying to have fun during a very scary time. The well-known phrase, "laughter is the best medicine," actually comes from Proverbs 17:22 in the Bible. Here's the version I like best, from the Amplified Classic Bible:

A HAPPY HEART IS GOOD MEDICINE,
AND A CHEERFUL MIND WORKS HEALING,
BUT A BROKEN SPIRIT DRIES UP THE BONES.

This statement has been proven over and over again. Happy, grateful people tend to be healthier. You can laugh your way to health. Laughter and gratitude can keep away negativity, which can lead to sadness and depression. It also helps your body to heal physically.

DEFENSE STRATEGIES TO RISE AGAIN

People constantly tell you what you should and shouldn't do, but not many people tell you what you can be! These tips are great defense strategies that will help you to rise again. *RESURGAM*.

- Be preventative rather than reactionary
- Be more responsible for your own health needs and act upon them
- Be aware of your personal history and triggers

- Be aware of mental, physical, and emotional fatigue
- Be stricter with your time management and boundaries
- Be honest with yourself
- Be more attentive to your own needs
- Be kind to yourself.
- Be educated – Information = hope
- Be fun and grateful!

HAPPY, GRATEFUL PEOPLE TEND
TO BE HEALTHIER. LAUGHTER AND
GRATITUDE HELP YOU BETTER COPE
WITH TRAUMA AND STRESS.

EIGHT

WHAT YOU DON'T KNOW CAN HURT YOU

One of the biggest challenges many people have is not knowing when they need help. If they do figure that out, it's often hard to know what type of help is needed, what's available, and where to find it, especially if their brain has shut down following a critical event and they just can't think straight. Another problem is that people may recognize that they need help, but those they look to for that help aren't able or qualified to help in the right way. At the beginning of this book, I shared my experience about how my sergeant didn't recognize acute stress in me. Had it been addressed earlier and properly, it would have probably allowed me to have a full and enjoyable career with the correct care. In no way do I blame him because, in those days, this subject was still misunderstood and, in my police department, very much taboo. My emotional and mental health is my responsibility. Yours is your responsibility. We can't blame other people or failed systems if we don't ask for help in the first place.

When I was in the police, the stress that came with the job was often ignored and brushed under the carpet. Sadly, we frequently still see this kind of lack of support in many career fields. This is true especially in fire and police departments, the medical field, pastoring churches, and other highly stressful jobs. Thankfully the tide is turning, and there's certainly an increased level of awareness and wonderful support for people experiencing acute distress or trauma. But how does all of this affect you? Especially if you don't fit into any of the high-stress career categories above. Let me answer that with some more questions.

THOSE IN ACUTE DISTRESS OR TRAUMA DESERVE SUPPORT AND UNDERSTANDING.

Have you ever been in physical pain but ignored it, thinking it would go away? You waited and waited, hoping to get better, and after some time, you finally seek medical help, only to find out that you're sicker than you realized. Had you gone to the doctor sooner, you may not have been as sick as you were. You could have avoided the strong medicines you're now taking or the surgery you needed because too much damage was done. Are you the kind of person that never looks at instructions when putting together a new piece of furniture? If you'd have checked the instructions, you may have finished the project an hour earlier, and you wouldn't have any leftover unused pieces. Are you the type of person who never asks for directions even when you're late to an appointment because you're convinced you can still find your way despite the fact that you're driving down the wrong road? Or have you ever been driving along, enjoying a road trip in an unfamiliar area when you lose cell service or your GPS stops working? Sure, we all have. Sometimes not knowing the way or the instructions to do something can either increase the fun of the adventure, or it can be frustrating or even scary if you're seriously lost.

GETTING LOST IS EASY WITHOUT CLEAR MARKERS

This happened to Rob and me last year. We went on a hike, one we hadn't done before. This particular hiking area had great reviews about new trails that had just been opened to extend the hiking adventures and distances. We picked a trail that would only take about an hour since we didn't have much time that day. It was certainly beautiful—lots of hills and thickly forested areas and, at first, very well signed trails. After laughing and joking along the way and allowing the signs to direct us on what we thought was a looped hike, we began to notice that trail signs were missing at some of the trail forks. If there were signs, they were confusing. At one place, they pointed us to the left to return to base, but there were two left turns. At that junction, it wasn't clear which one to take.

After some time, we noticed that we'd already been out for more than an hour and hadn't reached the parking lot. When we got to the next trail junction, convinced that it would take too long to backtrack, we chose one of two badly marked left turns, and off we went. This happened more than once, and before long, we were completely lost, yet we were having a great time just exploring. Soon we'd been hiking for two hours and had no idea where we were, but we weren't too worried—yet. The trails were all around us, several of them with multiple options at each junction but with no signs, so we just kept turning left, thinking we'd eventually circle back to base. Wrong! Another hour went by, and the sun was beginning to set. We hadn't seen another human being for a very long time, so there was no one to ask for directions. The park closed at 5 pm, so if we didn't get back to our car in time, we'd be locked in for the night.

We tried to use the GPS on Rob's phone and the trail app on mine to have two references for direction. One for the overall view of the area and the other for the actual directions. But the trails were so new that the trail app hadn't been updated, and the GPS just showed us being in the middle of a big green patch on the screen. We could figure out the general area where the car was parked, but each time we made a turn in that direction, the path didn't go the way we needed it to because of switchbacks or other roadblocks, such as a big ravine, a very deep muddy area and big fences that we couldn't cross. Before long, both of our phone batteries died because the apps and GPS drained them. We'd been checking them regularly to see if they'd give us updated information from different parts of the park. It was getting darker, and we were quickly losing the ability to see where we were going clearly. We couldn't use our flashlights on our phones, so we gave up on trying to find our way back to the car and just headed toward the sound of traffic on a road that we believed to be nearby. It wasn't as close as we'd hoped.

After what seemed like a very long time, we finally emerged from the forest onto a quiet country road. But where were we? We were seriously lost, and there weren't any street lights this far out of town. We didn't even know what time it was because we rely on our phones instead of wearing watches. Needless to say, we did eventually find our way back to the car and got out of the park with literally five minutes to spare, and it was very dark by then.

WHAT YOU DON'T KNOW CAN HURT YOU

BETTER INFORMATION ALLOWS FOR BETTER DECISIONS

The whole point I'm making is that had we known what we now know about that specific hiking area, we would have made different choices. We didn't know that many of the new trails were badly marked or unmarked altogether. Had we known, we wouldn't have chosen that hike because we'd have understood that we'd probably get lost. That's never good on any hike. We didn't know that there were so many new trails interlinking at various spots, which made finding our way out really hard. It was like a maze! We didn't know that our one-hour hike would turn into a four-hour hike, meaning that we were hiking in the dark at the end of the day and nearly got locked in the park all night. We didn't know that our phones would die so fast. Thankfully we were close to home, and everything worked out well, but had we been hiking somewhere more dangerous, this could have ended badly.

One winter, Mum was really sick with a chest infection for several weeks. At first, she didn't do anything about it because she thought she had a bad cold that had gone to her chest. After a couple of weeks of this, she eventually saw her doctor, who treated her with different rounds of antibiotics, but they weren't helping. At the time, I remember thinking that had she gone in sooner, the infection wouldn't have been so bad. A few more weeks went by, and eventually, they did a chest x-ray and told her she had pneumonia, so they changed her treatment plan accordingly. Time went on, and she still wasn't any better. After more tests and several weeks later, we heard the awful news that she had lung cancer. From memory, this all took about three months from when she first got sick to the cancer diagnosis. This is a good example of damage being done due to Mum and her doctors not knowing the facts, therefore not taking action earlier. What they didn't know did hurt her because they didn't know why she was really sick until it was too late. Neither Mum nor her doctor had the facts, and it had serious consequences. Ultimately the cancer killed her.

This wasn't a time for what if, should've, would've, or could've. But, had she been diagnosed sooner, the outcome may have been very different. Similarly, before I was diagnosed, the radiology office told my GP and me that my mammogram was clear, but I knew something was wrong. They didn't have the facts and misdiagnosed me, and my doctor believed them. She thought she had the facts, but the information she'd been given was wrong. It wasn't until I kept pushing for more tests that they changed their diagnosis of me, and my oncology treatment started quickly. So again, what they didn't know at first, could have been fatal for me.

BE SURE YOUR INFORMATION IS RELIABLE

I'm not trying to be a scaremonger here or a Debbie-downer. I know that there are always times when we just ignore things because we're busy and plan to take care of them later. I also appreciate that not everything is so serious that we always have to go on fact-finding missions. I'm saying that some things that we don't know could potentially be harmful to us in many ways. Sometimes we think we know more than we actually do. We think we have all of the facts about situations we're in, and the truth is that it's impossible to have all of the facts if we have no idea what questions to ask in the first place. We tend to make health choices based on what we think we know, proving that what we don't know can sometimes hurt us. If we don't use the support, instructions, help, or directions available to us, or if the appropriate, helpful resources we need aren't there for us, it usually ends up causing issues that could otherwise be avoided.

BE WILLING TO ASK FOR HELP

I want to encourage you to think about times when you may need to ask for help, either now or in the future. What about being willing to ask for help at times when you may feel it's silly or unnecessary? If there is anything in your heart or mind causing you concern, don't try to push through on your own to the point of neglect or harm. Obviously, there needs to be a balance between being a hypochondriac and a stubborn old goat, but I'm trying to encourage those of you who suffer in silence to stop doing that. There is no shame in reaching out, ever!

> SUFFERING IN SILENCE IS NOT VIRTUOUS. THERE IS NO SHAME IN REACHING OUT FOR HELP.

How does this tie into self-care, though? The whole point of self-care is to give yourself permission to be kind to *you*, for once. We've all been raised to believe it's okay to leave our needs out until we've cared for everyone else first. Yes, that is true at times because it's good to be hospitable, loving, and show kindness to others, but it's not okay to do this at the expense of our own well-being.

Do you think it's okay to cause harm to other people in any way? Should we get away with injuring others mentally, emotionally, physically, or spiritually, which could lead to their unhealthy behavioral responses? No, of course not. So why do we think it's okay to do it to ourselves? Seriously! We constantly harm ourselves by not making choices we need to make to protect ourselves in every area that we have the right to protect. We often do it without thinking about it. It's an automatic reaction that we're so used to doing that it doesn't occur to us that it's unhealthy or just plain wrong. Remember boundaries? What boundaries must you establish for your well-being? Is it right for you to treat yourself as nicely as you treat others? Actually, no. It's not. What?? I can imagine you all doing a double-take right now. Why isn't it right for you to treat yourselves as kindly as you'd treat others? Because I strongly believe that you actually should treat yourself **_better_** than you treat others in these areas.

You have full and sole responsibility for yourself. You must care for your own body, mind, emotions, soul, and spirit. No one else will do it for you. You have a duty to do what you must, to enable yourself to live life to the fullest by doing what you can to work through the hardships you'll face from time to time. I understand and respect that I have no idea how easy or hard your life is right now: how healthy or sick you are, what your financial situation is, whether you have a job or not, a home or food in your fridge.

> YOU HAVE FULL AND SOLE RESPONSIBILITY TO CARE FOR YOURSELF.

I've been through all of those challenges and yet still know that there are things I can do to make sure I still emerge as well-balanced and healthy as I possibly can. As parents, we care for our children by making sure they eat healthy food, dress warmly, drink plenty of water (instead of too much soda, tea, and coffee). We ensure they're in bed on time, so they get plenty of rest. We make them play outside in the fresh air and not spend too much time staring at screens ... and yet we think our bodies, minds, and emotions will survive on different rules. Let me tell you something; they won't.

CARE FOR YOUR NEEDS

Even Jesus encouraged the disciples to step away from ministry from time to time to put their needs first. They were being followed by crowds of people, all desperate to connect with them for different reasons. When I would read of Jesus walking away from hurting people who desperately needed Him to heal them or be taught by Him, I'd sometimes feel indignant towards Him because I felt He was being unkind and unloving. It wasn't until I started learning all that I now know, and all that I'm sharing with you today, that I learned a valuable lesson from Him. And that is, it's okay to walk away when you're running on empty. In fact, it's the best thing to do for your sanity and health. Please reassess your needs and permit yourself to make the necessary adjustments you need to keep your sanity and strength up. Others depend on you to be the best you can be; do this for their sakes too. Your families, your church, your work colleagues and clients, your friends, and most importantly, you yourself all need you around for a very long time. They all need you to be healthy, vibrant, strong, and happy. All of this is fully your responsibility, so this is really all about you, and that's okay!

Mark 6:30-32 says: "The apostles [sent out as missionaries] came back and gathered together to Jesus, and told Him all that they had done and taught. And He said to them, '[As for you] **come away by yourselves to a deserted place, and rest a while**'—for many were [continually] coming and going, and they had not even leisure enough to eat.² And they went away in a boat to a solitary place by themselves.

You can see that the disciples had just returned from ministering to many people because they'd been sent out as missionaries. We have no idea how long they'd been away for, but when they got back, they were hungry and tired and were telling Jesus all that they'd done. What's the first thing Jesus said to them? Can you see how he teaches them about self-care? We can clearly see that many people were still desperate to be ministered to in this passage because it says that Jesus told the disciples to come away to a deserted place, a quiet private place. Why? Because they needed to rest for a while and hadn't eaten for a long time!

What's He saying here? He's telling them that there will always be plenty of work to do, plenty of people who need you. There's always another "to do" list to get through, time frames to meet, and chores to do, but if you don't take a break, get away from everything that's pulling at your time, attention and energy, to refresh, feed your body, mind, and soul, you won't last long. They went away to a solitary place, a private place where no one could disturb them. How often do you give yourself permission to do that? To withdraw and have some quiet time, some "me" time? It is vital to your survival in this world if you want to finish well. Jesus did, so you can too.

KEEP YOUR TANK FULL

Let's imagine that you're like a gas tank with holes in your side, and every time you're filled up with reserves, which is your energy or fuel, the fuel leaks out of the holes. Every morning when you wake up, if you've slept well, you're full of the fuel of energy and life. Once you start going through your day, you leak out of the holes, and the more you leak, the less fuel you have, resulting in less energy to keep you running efficiently in the five main areas on which we've been focusing. By the end of the day, you're empty, running on fumes, and there's nothing left to give to anyone. Now, some things will make you leak faster, and if those happen, you'll be empty before lunch. You can also do things to make yourself leak more slowly so that you're still filled with energy and fuel at the end of the day. The things that make you leak and drain faster are the things that stress you out. The bigger the stress, the more you leak. Do you remember when we discussed eustress and distress? Well, let's think of the distressful things in your life that drain your energy reserves, such as having to deal with unreasonable deadlines at work or a grumpy boss. What about kids that don't do their school work on time or teens that don't come home on time. It could be that you're behind on paying the bills or that you're stuck in bed feeling sick. Anything that distresses you will drain your tank faster than usual.

All of the things that help to refill your fuel tank are the eustress things in your life, the positive stressors that energize you, bring you joy, and keep you focused, such as having a promotion that you've worked hard for, or having a baby, going on holiday or having your best friend come to stay. Now, the trick is this. Make sure you have enough eustress and positive things in your life to balance out the distress. In other words, keep filling your tank with things that bring you joy and strength to keep going, especially when it comes to having favorite pastimes and hobbies like going for a walk, having a massage, playing games with friends, playing your favorite sport, having a date with someone special, reading a book or taking a nap in the middle of the day and getting to bed on time. All of those things are vital to your mental health and well-being, and they'll help fulfill you and keep you healthy emotionally, physically, and spiritually.

Your behavior will automatically follow suit and improve if those other areas are well filled with fun activities, ideas, and thoughts. These things will fall in line with the same concept that Jesus was teaching His disciples in Mark 6. You must care for yourself if you're expecting to stay healthy and keep going long term, whether at work, in ministry, and at home as parents, husbands, or wives too, especially if you want a long, healthy, and active life.

THE BIBLE SUPPORTS SELF-CARE

Let's revisit the importance of sleep. Do you generally sleep well? If not, did you know that God gives you blessings as you sleep? If you didn't know that, I suspect the subject of sleep is another area where you may be causing harm to yourself by not knowing this simple fact from the Bible. Do you find yourself waking up too early or lying awake at night fretting about things? Psalm 127:2 says. **"It is vain for you to rise up early, to take rest late, to eat the bread of [anxious] toil, for He gives [blessings] to His beloved in sleep."** In other words, permit yourself to sleep as much as you can and don't get up earlier than necessary. Go to bed on time and try not to be anxious about things because that anxiety keeps you awake. If you trust that God's able to meet all of your needs, you'll find it easier to rest well because His blessings come to you as you sleep. What are His blessings? Well, He knows what you need more than you do, so trust Him with your worries and concerns, and He will be faithful to care for you, to provide the answers you need, and carry you through the dark days. Now that you know that, please be encouraged to make different choices about your sleep habits and any potential anxiety.

Why do you think the Bible gives us self-care advice? Why does Jesus tell His disciples to rest and eat? Why does He tell us that He's come to heal the sick, give sight to the blind, and set the captive free? It's because He knows we all need help in these areas. Unless we're physically sick or injured and end up needing medical attention, we're all generally really bad at recognizing when something is wrong with us physically, mentally, emotionally, spiritually, or behaviorally.

When we don't recognize that something is wrong, we don't know that we need help, and even if we are fortunate enough to figure that out, we don't always know what kind of help we need or what support systems are available to us. Therefore, we tend not to ask for the help we truly need in a crisis. If we don't know about it and don't request it, we can do ourselves harm. It's always better to be safe than sorry, so reach out at any time that you need extra help, even if you are unsure if it will help or not.

I may sound like a broken record, but so many people roll their eyes at the subject of self-care, or healthy defensive habits, such as the ones we discussed in the last chapter. But if you don't pay attention and learn about these things, what you don't know will hurt you. Not today, maybe, or tomorrow, but it will happen at some point, so you must make choices for your life that you need to make to keep yourself healthy in every way. Please pay attention to all of the signs and symptoms of mild stress, eustress, acute stress, and trauma that I've mentioned. Assess your responses to stressful situations because the ones I've already described aren't necessarily the only ones you may experience.

On the other hand, you may not experience any of the ones I've mentioned but could experience different symptoms. Either way, remember that your body, mind, and soul are unique. Learn to listen to your feelings and needs in those areas, and pay attention to them, trust them. Becoming more in tune with your inner being is a vital part of your strategy. It provides defensive ways to protect and allow yourself to recover from difficult events. Be kind to yourself, even generous. Value yourself because you are indeed valuable. Show yourself some

YOUR BODY, MIND, AND SOUL ARE UNIQUE. LEARN TO LISTEN TO THEM.

respect. Find out what resources are available to you. Give yourself permission to take as much time as you need to rest, regroup, recover, and decide what you need at this moment, putting up boundaries if necessary. Use the resources around you in those difficult times as much as you can. Seek out resources such as friends, family, neighbors, even going to a counselor for a short while, or seeing your doctor to obtain helpful medications if necessary.

NATURAL ALTERNATIVES

Another area where "what you don't know will hurt you" is in the area of natural alternatives. I'd encourage everyone to see a naturopath as well as other resources. If you're beginning to recognize that over the years you've not been as kind to your body as you should have been or want to be now, seeing a naturopath is a great start. Some medical doctors are too quick to give you medicines in the form of synthetic compounds, even chemicals in various forms to treat the symptoms you're battling with, but that doesn't get to the root cause of the problem. I'll stick my neck out here by saying that, in my opinion, some medications are handed out much too frequently to cover symptoms or make them disappear for weeks, months, or even years on end. But there is another way. Not for everything, I agree, but for most things.

A naturopath is a great resource for helping you get to the root causes of your physical issues and treating the causes, not masking the symptoms. There is a huge difference. A good naturopath will help you get yourself back into homeostasis physically by adjusting your diet to non-GMO and preferably organic food sources and suggesting natural, high-quality supplements. You'd be surprised how much your mental state and emotions automatically adjust to being more stable and even feeling better when your body is given the right foods and healthy natural supplements, rather than some other alternatives out there. Remember my comments about buying organic foods, if possible, rather than the cheapest option out there? Well, the same goes for supplements. Just because you buy multivitamins doesn't mean that the quality of the ingredients in that pill or powder is high enough to do any good. Some are cheap knock-offs of the real thing. Get information, get educated. Learn which brands are actually worth spending the money on.

PEER SUPPORT

Having peer support is a very effective way to manage acute stress. Many organizations now have peer support teams made up of well trained and trusted work colleagues that you can go to when you need someone to talk to. Joining support groups and reaching out to your social groups or your church for help are also good ideas. Remember that education is gathering information, and information brings hope. I'm trying to educate you in all of this so that you have a wide spectrum of resources and ideas to manage your well-being in many ways but yes, a lot of this all ties back to how you treat your body through diet, sleep, exercise and good hydration. If your body is stressed out due to you not understanding how to care for it, you run the risk of causing yourself more harm because of what you didn't know.

THERE IS ALWAYS HOPE

The question is, what are you going to do with all of this new information? It's up to you. No one else will make the choices you need to make for yourself. Your responsibility is to get educated, make constant assessments, and put your needs first in these areas. If you're experiencing hard times in any area right now and if what I'm saying is touching a nerve, I want to encourage you to not accept your current situation as being "just the way it is." There is always hope, always the chance of a better way to do things. Please don't just believe that what you currently know is all there is to know or that you already have all of the facts. There could be more information, more truths, that once revealed, could lead you on a different road, a healthier and happier road, so please reach out and get whatever support you need so that you can and will rise again. ***RESURGAM!***

NINE

THE TRAUMA OF GUILT AND SHAME

⋖⋗ ଓ ଓ ଓ ⋖⋗

Numb. Frozen in time. The sounds in our office faded as my brain tried to tell me that what I just saw on my desk was really true. Is this April Fool's Day? If so, this is a cruel joke, but it wasn't a joke, nor was it April 1ˢᵗ. With utter disbelief, I stared at the crime report. Everything inside me shut down, and I fought to hold back the tears. My stomach retched, and I desperately tried to compose myself, but how could this be? There's no way ...

"Fran...FRAN!" I snapped to. My colleague was telling me about the male body found in the river. He had jumped off

a very high local bridge. Other officers came into our Crime Prevention office to discuss the facts of the case with us. A huge investigation began the evening before, and it was about to rip the town apart. It certainly ripped me apart. Grief, shock, and utter confusion hit me at the same time. My mind spun with so many questions. Are you really gone? Why didn't you come to us or say something? Why didn't you ask for help? Surely nothing was so bad that you had to take your own life? Why did you jump? Why did you choose that particular bridge? What the hell happened!!??

As my colleagues talked, I was still frozen. It was as if the world was moving on, and I was stuck, still trying to get a grip and pull myself together for fear of letting my colleagues see what was really going on in me. The shock, shame, guilt, and grief were all rising up fast, and I had nowhere to go. I couldn't run. I couldn't escape, and neither could I show my colleagues my reactions.

In typical cop fashion, the conversation quickly turned from being about the severity of the case to cracking jokes, to deal with the disgust they felt at the things the man had done - to little boys. I was in so much turmoil. I could barely stay in the room, but I had to. One of my jobs was to collate all of the daily crime reports for crime pattern analysis and give them to the Chief Inspector each week, and this report was on top of the pile. No escape; everyone was standing between my desk and the door in the small office. I sat down and tried to work. I read the report over and over again, trying to find something that I might have missed. Something that told me that this wasn't really his body. Not really his car found on the bridge. Not my friend!

He and his family were close friends of ours. Just before that tragic day, we'd had them over for supper. We enjoyed a lovely meal followed by playing board games. We loved them dearly, and their sons were our sons' ages. He was engaging, fun, talented, and very passionate about teaching music to young children. He played the organ in our church; he was a dearly loved member of our community, a school teacher, and a local choir director. Our boys were in the choir that he taught and led. They went on choir trips with him, and we trusted him with our boys' lives. Literally, there were never any signs that he couldn't be trusted with them.

I struggled with guilt. How did I not know? How did I miss this? Why didn't I see the signs? How could I put my boys in danger like this? Then shame hit me, and I was filled with fear that if the other officers knew I was friends with him, they'd question my integrity too. I couldn't let them see how ashamed, upset and angry I felt. Ashamed that they'd judge me if they knew how much I cared for my friend, despite the fact that he'd been arrested the night before for something awful, inconceivable, and disgusting. Confused because he wasn't who I thought he was. Angry that he'd done what he was accused of doing and angry that he'd taken his life without asking for help first. Upset that there was nothing I could do at that moment other than just get to work and deal with the paperwork in front of me without letting anyone know that inside, my heart was ripping out of my chest, and I was barely holding it together.

My friend was highly revered in the community and had been heavily involved in choral music throughout England and other parts of Europe too. It was brutally painful for his amazing wife and sons, who knew nothing of his dark secrets or addiction. News of his death rippled further afield than anyone believed it would and affected more communities than thought possible. He taught at several schools and was in more than one choral group. Too many questions were asked surrounding the circumstances of his death. Rumors and tongue-wagging caused more pain to so many. My colleagues at the police station continued to investigate for some time as other boys came forward to share their testimonies. Thankfully my boys weren't among them. Even to this day, they say they never suspected a thing.

It was brutally painful for so many people for a variety of reasons. The choral society was split between those that loved and missed him and those that suddenly hated him for the crimes he committed on their sons, and who can blame them? Not to mention the fact that he and his family attended our church. How did the church deal with it? There was silence, or so it seemed, but it was a long time ago, and we did things differently back then.

It's been over 20 years since this tragic time, and even after so much time has passed, I still dread going over that bridge on my way home. Literally, dread it, and wish I could avoid it, but there's no other route to take. I'm still grieving even now. Grieving the loss of my friend, grieving the fact that he took his life, that he didn't ask for help, that he was so riddled with guilt and shame that he couldn't face the consequences of his actions. I grieved the loss of who I thought he was and the loss of how the music and choral communities once thrived under his leadership. The trauma of that time and the memories of my reaction when I saw the report on my desk are still fresh. My throat tightens, I go silent, and I think of him, his wife, his precious sons and wish for a different outcome.

༺ ༉ ༉ ༉ ༺

I shared that particular story to demonstrate how one man's choices and tragic suicide impacted a large, very diverse group of people over a wide geographical area. The ripple effects were strong and surprising. His story leads us into the topic of how to help others in trauma. Most of this book has been about you, which is fine because at the end of the day, it is, in fact, all about you, and that's okay! It was meant to be because you're invaluable—to God, to your circle of friends and family, and to others you haven't met yet. Whether you believe in God or not, I'm confident that you have a destiny, planned out by Him, for an amazing life and future, which will touch and impact those lives that you haven't crossed paths with yet. But to get there, you need to assess and adjust along the way to stay on the right path and head in the right direction so that your path actually does cross with the people you're meant to meet along the way. Yes, you'll get knocked off the path, knocked off your feet, but don't stay there. Pick yourself up, dust yourself off because you've been created to rise again to greet the next day – people are waiting to meet you and to know what you now know. People who need you to take them by the hand, pull them up, and help them rise again, just as I am helping you now.

I'm often called in to help a church, a family, an individual, or a community deal with trauma, and I'm passionate about being able to do that. Many others do what I do, but we need far more people to be trained in trauma response as well as spiritual and emotional care. I firmly believe that all of the things I've shared in this book are basic life skills that everyone should have. They can be the difference between life or death, not just physically but mentally, emotionally, behaviorally, or spiritually. They're not just for you, so you can assess your own needs, as we've discussed in-depth because it doesn't stop there. Remember when I spoke about how nothing gets wasted, ever? Well, here's where we'll look at what's next because I want to encourage you to use what you've learned to help others.

Everything I've shared with you in this book are life-skills that you now have with you 24/7 from this day forward. My goal is that all of this new knowledge will stay with you, to be used daily, not only for your benefit but for the benefit of all those around you. You'll be surprised at how your newfound knowledge will quicken your antennae when others around you are struggling and don't know what to do. Hopefully, you'll have compassion for them. That compassion, along with your new confidence, can help make a huge difference in their lives. You can prevent them from hurting themselves due to what they don't know. With that being said, let's look at other ways to help you with that: what to look out for, how you can be a lifeline between someone in trauma, and help them connect with the resources they need.

THE TOLL OF HIGH-STRESS JOBS

Over recent years the suicide rate of pastors, doctors, nurses, firefighters, and police officers has drastically increased. I'm not saying that suicide rates in other careers or social circles are less important, but these are the main groups I'm connected with in my work. One suicide is one too many. It's a tragic end to a precious life that has ripple effects that aren't known or realized until it's too late. I want to encourage you to think about the story I just shared. As I watched this tragedy unfold, I was stunned at how far-reaching the implications were, even many years later. Not only were there repercussions of one man's destructive choice to sexually abuse young boys, but also the resulting consequences because of his choice to take his own life and destroy his family. This discussion right now is not about our personal opinions of him or what he did. It's about the facts of how his choices affected other people's lives. He was a husband, father, teacher, friend, son, brother, and loved by many. He was such a high profile and greatly appreciated influence in our town and the country's choral community. He was charming, engaging, brilliantly musical, and passionate about teaching others what he knew and his influence went far and wide in those wonderfully gifted and generous areas. Yet, no one knew what went on in his mind, in his heart, in secret. No one knew of the things going on behind closed doors.

What we didn't know hurt us as a community and also hurt many individuals. His secret life brought death, destruction, trauma, grief and had long-lasting effects. It changed his family, the families of those he abused, the various communities he worked in, and our town forever. In many ways, he's no different than you and me. We all have a secret life about which we feel guilty. We all have shameful issues we struggle with and try to keep hidden for fear that we'd be cast out, rejected, abandoned, or ridiculed if anyone saw who we really were. But that's where the danger lies. We must overcome those strong fears by believing that we're lovable and valuable enough to be real, transparent. We need to find someone with whom we feel safe, someone we will allow into our emotional "home," our intimate inner boundary. We should ask for help before it gets out of hand and leaks out, ending in our destruction. On the other side of that coin is how you should treat others who struggle with guilt and shame. If you truly want to help them, you must let them know that they're safe with you. Please do all you can to help them, without reacting unprofessionally or unkindly. If they're entrusting you with their pain and heart, be fully trustworthy and committed to helping them rise again to health and wholeness.

DEFINING GUILT

We need to look at guilt and shame before we go any further. Why? Mentally and emotionally, those two factors cause more damage than we realize. I really want to spend some time here looking at these two words, their etymology, meaning, and how they affect us all. They play a large part in your life and, therefore, will also play a large part in the lives of those you'll be able to help in the future. I need you to understand the role they play, especially in trauma. These emotions are strong and are very common ones that I know you've already experienced, but they're hard to unravel. You need to understand a little more about how they affect you and those you'll come across as you help others.

I did absolutely nothing wrong when my friend died. I didn't know what choices he was making. I didn't help him in his abuse of boys. I didn't encourage him to take his own life, and yet on that painful day when I saw the report on my desk, you'll remember that I was riddled with guilt and shame, but why? I felt ashamed because I was embarrassed, shocked, angry, and hurt by what he had done. He was also a friend of mine, one I was very fond of, and I was utterly devastated that he was dead. Rightly or wrongly, I dreaded anyone knowing that he was my friend or that I felt the way I did because my feelings didn't match their reactions towards him. He had committed a crime that society disdains, and I know that's putting it mildly. I felt guilty just by association. That guilt led to the feelings of shame that they'd discover that I was grieved by the loss of someone I cared about. In their eyes, he was someone who'd abused children, and they were right, but so was I. Some of the officers weren't speaking kindly or nicely about him in the office that morning (or for several weeks after the fact). I understood why, but my choices on that particular day were to join in with the unkind conversations or just keep my mouth shut. I kept my mouth shut and desperately longed for them to leave the office so that I could break down and cry. I was in deep grief and trauma as a result of this. No one could know how I felt. I had to protect myself from them finding out the truth, so I shoved the pain down and suffered in silence. Struggling with all of those emotions messed me up for weeks. Every time I went to work, I struggled with it. Even our church didn't handle it well; they didn't know how to, and in those days, neither did I. I shared all that to give you an idea of how someone can react to something they're not responsible for, purely due to guilt and shame, which means that you don't have to be guilty to feel the emotion of guilt. You don't have to have done something to be ashamed of, to feel ashamed.

YOU DON'T HAVE TO BE GUILTY TO FEEL THE EMOTION OF GUILT OR HAVE DONE SOMETHING WRONG TO FEEL ASHAMED.

The other major factor of guilt and shame that I also struggled with was that I had absolutely no clue what to do to help his wife, who was also my friend. How do I help his children or other close friends who were also traumatically impacted in so many ways? I felt awful! Have you ever had a friend who's going through a really painful time and you long to help but just have no idea of what to do, or say, or how to make any difference in their situation? Or have you been part of a community that's experienced a tragedy, and you struggled with feelings of guilt because you didn't know what to do? It can make you avoid those you want to help because you feel guilty or ashamed that you just don't know what to do. You're not alone, but hopefully, now you'll have the confidence to engage with them. I've shared many aspects of the signs and symptoms of trauma. By the end of this book, you'll also have a great idea of what to do to help them.

Another aspect of guilt you may come across is called survivor's guilt. This is guilt felt by someone who struggles with the fact that they survived something that someone else didn't. Usually, it happens when people experience the same deadly incident, like a car crash, a shooting, or a disaster, but only some survived. The survivors can get twisted up inside with guilt that they're still alive. They can become overwhelmed by thoughts of "why did they die but I didn't?" Or "it should have been me."

THE FEELING OF GUILT IS TIED TO YOUR EMOTIONS, WHEREAS BEING FOUND GUILTY BY LAW HAPPENS WHEN IT'S PROVED THAT YOU COMMITED A CRIME.

The root of the word guilt comes from an old English word, "gylt," meaning having committed a crime, or an offense, a violation or other type of wrongdoing, against either moral or criminal law. But, please remember that culturally, or morally, we all have different beliefs and different laws, so what may be of moral failure or criminal offense to one may not be to another. Feeling guilty is very different from being found guilty of a

156

crime. The feeling of guilt is tied to your emotions, whereas being found guilty by law happens when it's proved that you committed a crime. Someone can commit a crime and never feel guilty about it. When you feel guilty about something, it's commonly because you've violated your own standards, which are based on your culture, country's laws, and personal beliefs. Violating your own standards begins as a thought or a desire that directly influences a choice made, then an action follows—the action of "doing" something wrong or not doing what was right. James 1:14-15 describes it this way (I added the underlined words for clarification): **¹⁴ But every person is tempted when he is drawn away, enticed and** baited by his own evil desire (lust, passions). **¹⁵ Then the evil desire, when it has conceived, gives birth to sin, and sin, when it is fully matured, (<u>when acted upon</u>), brings forth death.**

DEFINING SHAME

Guilt violates your personal standards, whereas shame, on the other hand, violates a community's standards. If you didn't care what others thought about you or your choices, your battle with shame wouldn't be as strong. This emotion attacks the very core of who you believe you are and who you want everyone else to think you are by assaulting you with manipulative and controlling inner self-talk about the frightening consequences of exposure. It is rooted in deep fear and brings very strong emotional reactions because your identity and integrity are both about to be ripped to shreds if anyone finds out about what you did or didn't do, what you believe or don't believe. Even who you voted for in the last presidential election!

One possible root word for shame in the old English is "scamu," which means disgrace, dishonor, and loss of esteem. What does that remind you of? It's what we talked about before, when Jesus said he'd come to preach the good news to the poor, which when translated included being poor of spirit, meaning being disgraced, having loss of honor or self-esteem. While both guilt and shame are emotions, shame is the one that kicks your survival brain into high gear.

Shame causes feelings of intense embarrassment and fear. Your cheeks flush, your heart pounds and, before you know it, you're in fight or flight mode, desperate to escape from the "threat" of being exposed, rejected, cast aside, and humiliated. This is a traumatic response to an emotion, my friends! Does that surprise you? On a stronger or milder scale, depending on the severity of the shame you're feeling, your body is literally experiencing the same feelings as if you're in trauma. Think back to a time when you felt shame to the point where you dreaded anyone finding out about a secret you tried to hide. Or remember a time when you were acutely embarrassed and compare it to a time when you received some very bad news that sucker-punched you. I think you'd agree with me that the feelings and responses your body goes through are similar. Don't you think it's interesting that the emotion of shame triggers your entire body to go on the defensive and can trigger the fight or flight mode in your brain, influencing your choices and your behavior?

Shame is an extremely powerful emotion because the flight or fight mode is an immediate physiological response to danger or the threat of danger. Although it's not a physical threat, it is a threat to your identity and integrity in the eyes of those around you—especially friends who you don't want to be exposed to for fear of rejection.

These responses to shame are all rooted in the fear of being unloved, abandoned, and not accepted by society, friends, family, and any other people in your life with whom you want to be in a relationship. The terrifying trap of guilt and shame can cause all of us to hide and to lock whatever it is that we're trying to keep under wraps so tightly that no one ever finds out the truth of what we've done or who we really are. I use the word "terrifying" here because when I've felt ashamed, the intense fear that someone might discover what I did or didn't do has been debilitating at times, to the point that it affected my choices, behavior, and mental health.

Out of guilt and shame, shame is the strongest and most controlling emotion. It can cripple us, causing every aspect of our behavior, belief systems, and choices to change overnight. It's rooted in guilt but exaggerated by fear. Guilt only comes as a result of two things. Either we've done something we feel we shouldn't have done, or someone else has done something to us that humiliates us, especially if we believe it's our fault in the first place. For example, if you're abused by someone else, the abuser is a controller, and most controllers, over time, can cause you to believe the lie that their treatment of you is a direct result of your behavior and choices, so it's your fault. Shame comes as a result of feeling guilty about something.

Guilt is the knowledge that we did something we shouldn't have done, but shame is the stronger emotion. It partners with guilt every time. Even if what we did wasn't wrong, but we believe that it was, the shame still keeps us bound, trapping us in a tight cocoon of self-preservation to the point that we begin to tell lies to protect ourselves. We cover up what we're hiding. Even if what we're hiding isn't considered as wrong or shameful to others, it's the shame that controls us. In its worst form, shame can lead to suicide, as it did with my friend. Suicide can result when someone reaches the place of being willing to do **anything** to stop the pain of having to walk through the consequences of your actions if you are found out.

TRUTH

Truth. That's a divisive word in a funny way because so many arguments happen over the truth of a matter. What is the truth? The real truth. I always say there are three sides to every story, every situation. There's your perspective or version of what happened or what was said, then there's my perspective or version, and in the middle is the absolute truth. Only one person in the entire world always knows all of the facts, the absolute truth in any situation, and that is God. He sees all and knows all and always has all of the facts and answers we could ever need.

In John 8:31-32, it says: "**So Jesus said to those Jews who had believed in Him, if you abide in My word [hold fast to My teachings and live in accordance with them], you are truly My disciples. And you will know the Truth, and the Truth will set you free**"

Being set free means being released from captivity, and Jesus came to set the captives free. What does this mean, though? How can the truth set someone free? First of all, when this passage says that we're to hold fast to Jesus's teachings and live by them, I know that this relates to so many different aspects of interpretation, ranging from being set free from sin by Jesus's death for us on the Cross to repenting of a sin which then releases you and sets you free from the guilt you carried. There are so many theological answers to those questions, but this book isn't about that, so we won't get into that here. This book aims to share what I have learned about acute stress, psychological trauma, and how to cope with it throughout my life. So, for now, we'll stick with that topic and talk about how God's truth helps us to manage our responses to painfully difficult situations the best way we can. Hopefully, we allow God's truth to set us free from the negative effects of traumatic events.

GOD'S TRUTH HELPS US TO MANAGE OUR RESPONSES TO PAINFULLY DIFFICULT SITUATIONS THE BEST WAY WE CAN.

I'm not a licensed therapist; however, I am highly trained. After many, many years of studying, attending, and teaching seminars, and practical application in the response field, I've learned enough to write this book. But the most impactful lessons I've learned have come from going through my own very dark days, my own experiences where I had to figure out what helped and what didn't. I spend time in prayer, studying the Bible, and finding out what God has to say to me about trauma, grief, sorrow, and learning what to do about it all—how to rise again from the death and destruction of trauma. That's how I adhere to His teachings about this topic. I choose to live in accordance with His truth by studying how He designed us, how He's intricately planned every cell in our body for a purpose, and wired us to respond to hard times in certain ways.

By implementing biblical teachings and the truths I've shared with you about trauma, your reactions to it, and what to do about it, I hope you're now being released from some misunderstandings you've possibly had surrounding this topic. The truths I've shared about self-care and incorporating defensive healthy habits will hopefully set you free from the incorrect choices that may have kept you captive in those areas until now. So, what now? What do I want you to do with all of this information? First, I want you to value yourself as I do. I, together with my fellow chaplains and trauma response colleagues, can't do this work alone. We need you! We need you to be the healthiest you can possibly be so that you live a long, happy, and healthy life, mentally, emotionally, physically, spiritually, and behaviorally. Why? Because you are worth it and because you can make a huge difference in this world. As you begin to rise up and heal in every area that we've talked about, there will come a time when you're strong and healthy enough to help others. To pay it forward. You have a responsibility to help others discover the same truths you're finding today. There are way too many wounded souls out there who need to hear what you now know.

SEEKING COMFORT AND HELP

It's a known fact that when a disaster hits a community or when a traumatic event severely affects an individual, those traumatized people reassess their beliefs, their faith, and search for a Higher Power—something or someone to bring them comfort and help them through the intense fear and pain. Church attendance always increases after disasters, but how does the church help those traumatized people get the help and support they need? We have to understand that by the time they finally reach out to the church for help, they're often fed up, exhausted, highly stressed, feeling as if the world has given up on them and they have nowhere else to turn. I firmly believe that church leadership should be well trained in understanding how to minister to people in trauma, both within the church family and within their communities. It doesn't matter who's in need. Sadly and wrongly, people have been excluded from being helped by many churches. A person's belief system, race, lifestyle choice, or other factors should not be considered. If somebody needs help and they turn to a church, surely that is the one place where they should be welcomed with open arms, lovingly helped, and put on a path to hope, health and recovery.

Many pastors and leaders either don't have the skills to recognize trauma and acute distress or they recognize the signs but don't always know what to do about it. Is this the pastor's fault? Is it the fault of the leadership or of the person asked to handle the need? No, not at all. Pastors and leaders of any faith group undergo training in reference to their positions, such as theology, church leadership, and so on. But in none of those classes are you likely to find information on how to help someone in emotional shock, intense grief, or trauma, such as I'm sharing in this book. As a general rule, we're still a long way off from having well-trained churches that understand how to help people in trauma. But it is slowly becoming something they are open to and about which they are learning.

Instead of receiving the correct help, too many times broken people just hear the phrases "I'll be praying for you," or "you can do all things through Jesus Christ who strengthens you," as a way to encourage them in their faith and with that they're shown out of the office. Those statements are biblically true in the Christian faith, and we are to pray for each other. Jesus can, and does, strengthen us. He enables us to do the things He's asking of us, but those phrases don't make sense if you're not of the Christian faith. They certainly aren't helpful when someone is in full-blown trauma! People don't need to hear scriptures and clichés that are thrown around, often glibly at times. They can sometimes do more harm than good. They're mostly used when well-meaning people don't know quite what to do or say. If you've heard these or similar phrases multiple times when going through a painful season, they can lose their value or meaning because they're not always said with sincerity. When someone is in trauma, they need emotional, mental, and physical help before anything else. Spiritual help is vital, of course. I firmly believe that for all of us, but it isn't the best place to start offering support. People don't usually want to hear about faith until they're well-fed, warm, hydrated, and supported in practical ways, and especially not until they feel safe and secure first and foremost.

A WORD TO PASTORS AND CHURCH LEADERS

These days many pastors themselves are increasingly under too much stress to pastor well and live healthy, balanced lives. The demands of pastoring are changing rapidly, and as mentioned before, suicide rates amongst pastors and church leaders are too high. At times, the decision to take one's life is caused by feelings of being overwhelmed with the pastoral responsibilities, which can lead to feelings of failure, followed by acute depression. I also strongly believe that those feelings tie into the strongholds of guilt and shame. I hope that many pastors will read this book and adopt some healthy habits and self-care ideas within its pages that apply to them. It is not only for their own well-being, but also for them to truly understand how to help those in their care. If you're a pastor or lay-leader reading this, I want to encourage you to lead by example. Please assess your own needs first, do your self-care, and establish healthy boundaries to protect your health in all areas because you carry heavy responsibilities.

Pastoring is full of blessings, joys, and fun times, but it's also exhausting, stressful, and painful, and since you don't have regular office hours, most of the time, it's a 24/7 job. As you lead by example, find ways to teach your church leadership and your congregation what you've learned. Don't keep it all to yourself because everyone needs to hear this freeing and life-changing information. Train your church in these skills so that as a church, you all share the load of responsibility to care for the needs of those in your church family and community. This type of work is very missional in its makeup because it gives you skills that, sadly, most people don't have. What better way to help the community than to care for their emotional, mental, physical, and behavioral well-being rather than just the spiritual?

WE CAN ALL HELP THOSE IN NEED

Please know that this isn't all about that group of people or about the Christian faith for those of you who aren't pastors and who don't attend a church. On the contrary, you're just as valuable and have just as important a role to play in helping others. Possibly a more difficult one because you need to position yourself in a place where people who need the tools and skills you now have can find you. People in a church are easy to find because if someone is looking for help, the church is a common place for them to go. But if you're not there, where can people in need go? After the Oso Mudslides in 2014 in Washington state, I helped local chuches set up a coffee shop as a drop-in center for people who just needed to talk to someone who was willing to listen. How can you make yourself accessible in a similar way?

This information should be taught in schools and colleges, especially when students' suicide rate is increasing. Can you make yourself available to schools as extra support to the school counselor? You'll certainly use these skills with your family and amongst your friends, but please think outside the box. There are plenty of places and people that need what you now have, so pay it forward. You'd be surprised at how many people you can help. You could let your

WHAT TO DO WHEN LIFE SUCKS

company know that you'd be willing to be a crisis responder at work for anyone struggling with the demands of a highly stressful job and intense deadlines. I know that many homeless shelters need people with these skills. Hospitals and assisted living shelters need volunteers to visit patients and residents who struggle with loneliness and the emotional issues caused by their ill health. The needs are never-ending. Everyone you meet has something going on in their lives that you can help them with.

> EVERYONE YOU MEET HAS SOMETHING GOING ON IN THEIR LIVES THAT YOU CAN HELP THEM WITH.

This shows them that they're valuable, worthy of love, of a listening, non-judgmental ear. Show them that you're a safe person for them to turn to for help. Help them rise again and have their own moment of *RESURGAM*.

TEN

PAY IT FORWARD

No matter who you are, where you live, what you do for work, or what you've been through, you can make a difference in other people's lives by sharing what you've learned so far. You can pay it forward by using your own life experiences. Remember, nothing is wasted, and you have the skills you've learned from this book. I'm confident that you'll now be able to recognize the tell-tale signs of stress, grief, or trauma in other people and bring comfort and encouragement that ministers to them just by being present. The ministry of presence means being there with them, offering support, and often without needing to say a word. Silence is okay. Let those you're comforting decide whether they want conversation or not. They'll definitely make it clear. They'll either talk freely or sit quietly, and the best thing is to let them choose.

PEOPLE IN STRESS RESPOND DIFFERENTLY

When people are hurting, conversation can be overwhelming. Sometimes, as I previously mentioned, people in distress or shock talk a lot, which you'll remember is called cathartic ventilation. It's a healthy and normal coping mechanism. Some people just want silence, and that's when your presence is enough. It's not always necessary to fill the silence with conversation. Just being with them, holding their hand, hugging them, offering silent support, and allowing them to talk if and when they feel like it is a huge gift. Please don't be a chatterbox if they need peace. If you notice that they're pulling away, don't worry, it doesn't necessarily mean you've done something wrong. They may need space, but it's nothing personal.

When under distress or trauma, energy levels can drop so much that people lack the emotional capacity to interact in the same way they usually do. You'll remember that they can quickly become very limited in what they're able to focus on or work on in the fight or flight mode. Their decision making is severely impacted, and their ability to process everyday things slows down. Their minds can even be so overwhelmed by the 'threat' of the circumstances that their brains just switch off and go blank. It's as if they've gone into mental hibernation.

Have you ever been so stressed that it feels as if someone has flipped a switch and turned your brain off? If so, you'll know from experience that there's absolutely nothing you can do about it other than relax, rest, and give yourself time to breathe. Better still, take a vacation. So, if you are trying to reach out and connect with someone who's going through a personally painful and emotional season, you may notice that they're not interacting with you as they usually do.

They may be kind and sweet as always but have pulled back a bit. They could be moody, impatient, distracted, and generally may treat you differently than they normally do. They may not be returning your phone calls, emails, or texts as fast as they have before. It could just be because they're very busy, and even though they do want to connect with you, they may need to wait until they can give you quality time. But, sometimes, it really is because they just don't have the capacity to talk to you for a while, but please do not take it personally. They truly may be unable to engage.

In times of acute stress, especially after losing a loved one, or diagnosis of a terminal illness, or too many deadlines, it's easy to be quickly overwhelmed with too many well-meaning communications. They don't have the mental or emotional capacity to engage on that level until their minds calm down and come out of the fight or flight mode, which can take a long time if the acute stress or trauma is ongoing. When I'm in that situation, I'm unable to have a conversation with anyone for longer than about fifteen minutes because my brain can't focus for longer than that. I feel it begins to shut off. It affects my hearing and my cognitive ability to think. Literally.

So, if you're in a relationship with someone who's overly stressed and not interacting with you the way you want them to, please remember this very important fact. **IT IS NOT ABOUT YOU!**

At that moment, they are trying to survive and are doing whatever they can do just to keep going, so please don't get offended. Don't start blaming or judging them just because they're not behaving the way you think they should. Your expectations at that moment aren't what's important. If you insist on them engaging with you, they may pull away because you're not respecting their boundaries. Your efforts to connect with them may put too much pressure on them, which depletes their ability to manage the emotional engagement of their relationship with you. It becomes an unhealthy cycle. Trust that they love you and want you in their life. Maybe just send them a note to let them know you're thinking of them. Offer to clean their house or make them a nice meal, without putting any expectations on them to do anything other than just receive your love. That will help them more than you know.

THE NEED FOR INFORMATION

Questions, questions, questions. We're always asking questions, especially if we're overwhelmed with intense emotions resulting from hearing bad news. Here's a tragic experience I went through in my late teens, which left me with questions that I didn't find answers to at the time, no matter how hard I tried.

✎ ❧ ❧ ❧ ✎

"He's dead," my friend said. "It was in the newspaper this morning."

"Don't tease me. That's not funny!" I replied, with a smirk on my face, thinking he was joking.

"I'm not teasing you, Fran. I saw it this morning. You go home and check for yourself."

As soon as I returned home, I ran to the kitchen. The daily paper was on the kitchen table, and there was the news I desperately hoped my friend had been teasing me about. I saw it, plastered on the front page, that a local soldier had been killed—by friendly fire! I froze. It was the first time I'd ever experienced my entire body instantly go numb. I was reading it again and again and again, trying to make sense of it. I couldn't move for what seemed like a long time. I saw his face smiling at me from the photo they chose of him in uniform. I'd never see that face again, or that smile. I was confused. Stunned. Too many questions flooded my mind. I needed to escape from the room where others milled around, to be alone. I could feel the tears coming but didn't want anyone to see them. As I got to my bedroom, where I planned to hide for a while, my mind still needing to make sense of what I didn't want to believe to be true. My knees buckled under me and my body hit the floor, sobbing. I cried off and on for several days. My eyes saw the news at that moment and tried to register in my mind, but it didn't make sense. How could this have happened? The war was already over!

I'd been talking to a friend that morning about the fact that the Falkland War was over, so the soldiers would be coming home. I was excited to see my soldier again, but I never did. Even as I write about this story from my teenage years, the tears are flowing. This is one of my most painful and tragic losses that still deeply hurt to this day, over 30 years later.

We didn't have cell phones, email, or any mode of quick correspondence then—only old rotary dial phones and telegrams. You couldn't Google everything to find all of the answers you needed, so there were no answers to the myriad of questions rattling around in my head, consuming me for a very long time. For years, in fact. What happened? Why did he die after the cease-fire? How did he get killed by friendly fire? Having no answers to those questions increased the pain of grief, of loss, more than you can imagine. If you've never experienced anything like this yourself, it's hard to describe. It's crushingly painful. In the efforts to constantly find answers, we go over the details again and again, desperately hoping that some new information would suddenly appear by doing so. But it doesn't, yet we keep searching because we long for the closure that never comes.

~৯ ঞ ঞ ঞ ঞ ~৯

If you're supporting someone who's just experienced something that causes them to have lots of questions about the circumstances, it's okay to try to get information on their behalf. People need facts. If you can find the answers to their questions, giving them the appropriate facts can bring a little comfort. Getting the facts is getting information. Obtaining the right kind of information brings hope, especially when that information is about any available resources or support, such as finding food, shelter, and supplies. You may offer help about where to find other kinds of care that may be needed, such as what happened and how to address the impact of what just happened, where to get financial support, or which therapist to see. Some people even need help deciding which funeral home would provide the best care and attention to a loved one who's just died.

People naturally search for the truth. What happened? Why did it happen? Who's involved? What to do about it? And other similar questions. If they can't find the answers they're looking for, their brain always fills in the missing pieces of information with the worst-case scenario details. Remember Mini-me working in your brain to file the information away in the appropriate cabinet? The brain has to be able to process the information it receives because it can't have loose ends flying about; no unfiled data. It always needs to put things away by finding the appropriate section in the correct filing cabinet. Filing it doesn't take away the pain or change the circumstances of what happened, but it can begin to calm down the mind and the emotions. By obtaining the necessary information for someone you're trying to help, you take the pressure off them, trying to fill the gaps.

> WHEN YOU OBTAIN INFORMATION FOR SOMEONE IN ACUTE STRESS, YOU TAKE THE PRESSURE OFF THEM CAUSED BY TRYING TO FILL IN THE GAPS.

Have you noticed how you always see in pictures? If you hear a story, you'll usually see it in picture form in your mind as you listen. That's how your brain functions. That's your imagination working on your behalf, putting information your mind receives into a picture file, so to speak, so that you can "see" it. When you hear traumatic news or information, your imagination fills in the missing pieces of information in pictures. Sometimes those pictures can be so graphic and frightening that those images cause more trauma. We can have overactive imaginations when we're upset, which is why we tend to assume the worst. That was my experience with the images in my head when my soldier died. My imagination went in far too many directions, and none of them were good for my emotions. If you're supporting someone who's lost a loved one, for example, and you have information surrounding the death that they don't have, you can help by giving them some information, but only if it's appropriate to share. Often giving them the answers they seek will calm them down. This is better than allowing their minds to run wild with imaginations that cause them more harm.

Use your common sense. If someone asks how their loved one died, they don't need all of the details if those details are likely to cause more trauma. You only give the facts as you know them. If in doubt about what to say, keep quiet. You can't take back words that have been spoken, and you certainly don't want to cause more harm.

RECOVERY TIMELINES AND "NEW NORMAL"

Remember when I explained that we wouldn't all find the same event as difficult to deal with as the next person due to the many variations in personality, training, experience, and so on? Well, it's just as important to remember that we'll also have different timelines of response to a crisis. Some people may experience their normal stress responses immediately, and for others, they'll come a few days or a week later. Some may not have any symptoms until later still, even as long as a few months. It goes without saying that we all have varying times of processing our reactions and beginning to manage our unique symptoms. When working with someone in acute stress or trauma, don't expect them to behave in a certain way or be "over" their grief by a certain time frame because it doesn't work that way. I don't even like the term "get over" anyway. People don't "get over" traumatic experiences. Instead, they learn to live with the consequences of the events and learn to manage their pain and their individual stress responses to them. Over time the pain does decrease, and their ability to cope with the aftermath increases. Everyone finds their own time frame to work within. But it's as individual a journey as you and I are individuals.

I'm sure you've often heard the term *new normal*. When supporting someone who's experienced something traumatic, it's common for them to begin to notice that the life they had before the major event, and the life after the event, are vastly different. The old self that they knew before the event has gone—has changed. You could even say the old self has died. That's how I feel each time I go through a significantly painful season. I was such a vastly different person after cancer. The old Fran had died, and the new, stronger, more determined, wiser, and more compassionate Fran emerged. At first, I didn't recognize myself because I processed my thoughts, emotions, and attitudes very differently after cancer. You may understand what I'm talking about if you've experienced it yourself. It's good to help others acknowledge that this is something they may be going through because it can feel confusing. I remember not feeling connected with my inner self for a long time. I didn't recognize my responses to things because they were so different from how the "old Fran" would have behaved.

It can be worrying to someone you're supporting who's unable to put their finger on what's happening to them when they notice they don't respond to life the same way anymore and that they don't process their emotions the same way. So, if you notice that, help them. Explain what's happening to them, that their new self is emerging and they're walking into a new existence, so to speak, figuring out what life looks and feels like now. Their old life, which is their pre-critical event life has gone. They now need to learn what their "new normal" life is all about. And that's all a normal part of their responses to abnormal events. But you need to help them through it because it doesn't feel normal. In fact, it can feel as if they're going crazy. Reassure them that they'll slowly adapt to their new life and encourage them that things can and do get easier.

WHEN IS IT TIME TO REFER THEM FOR QUALIFIED HELP?

When caring for others in trauma, it's important to know if and when to refer them to higher levels of care. We all experience post-traumatic stress, in other words, acute stress after a traumatic event, resulting in emotional, mental, physical, behavioral, or spiritual symptoms, similar to the ones I explained in chapter four. You'd expect some of those symptoms to begin to ease off within about 30-45 days, but if there's little or no improvement after that time frame, it's important to refer them to a therapist. There's a possibility that the post-traumatic stress may be so severe that it's become a disorder. Post-traumatic stress disorder (PTSD) is an injury that people definitely need to see a therapist for because only a therapist can actually diagnose PTSD. If they do have that, they'll need specialized care. The sooner they're diagnosed, the sooner their specialized care can start, providing the opportunity for better recovery. Unless you are a fully licensed mental health practitioner yourself, their care needs at that level are out of your realm of experience and expertise and certainly not something that anything in this book is qualified to help with.

AN UP-TO-DATE LIST OF GOOD THERAPISTS IN YOUR AREA THAT YOU CAN RECOMMEND IS AN IMPORTANT RESOURCE FOR YOU TO CULTIVATE. A very important resource that you'll need is an up-to-date list of good therapists in your area that you can recommend to the person you're helping. Please be careful to pay attention to what areas in which a therapist specializes. You wouldn't ask a carpenter to do your plumbing, would you? No, of course not, so please don't send a traumatized adult person to a child psychologist. Find a therapist that deals with trauma and, if possible, find one that's recommended to you by someone you trust. Another reason for finding a therapist to help them is that you mustn't be the only person supporting someone who's experienced a traumatic event. It's too big a burden for you to carry alone. Always ensure that you find other people, other resources to help share the burden of caring for them.

GRIEF

It's important to briefly mention a few other types of acute stress that you're likely to come across. We've discussed PTS and PTSD, but let's look a little more closely at grief. Grief is the emotional reaction to loss, and the depth of love and attachment to what was lost determines the intensity of grief felt, whether it was a loved one, a pet, house, job, dreams, hopes, or visions. Grief comes in layers of loss, meaning that you may notice that you grieve different aspects of the loss as you experience it. For example, if you lose a job that you love, you'll grieve that, but then you grieve the financial loss or security the job provided, followed by grieving the loss of friendships or connections at work that were important to you. Perceived loss also causes grief. You can start grieving the loss of something, or someone that you know will be gone soon.

COMPASSION FATIGUE AND BURNOUT

Two common types of emotional and mental exhaustion are compassion fatigue and burnout. I want to explain the difference between them. More people struggle with these two types of stress and exhaustion than is admitted. Both of these are shrouded in a lot of denial by those experiencing them, usually due to ignorance of not recognizing the issue.

Compassion fatigue is often easy to recognize because, as its name suggests, people lose their compassion for things they've been very compassionate about before due to exhaustion caused by caring for so many people over such a long period. It's commonly seen in people with careers requiring them to care for others, especially those whose work requires them to listen to many difficult stories and tragic tales. It's common for pastors, therapists, nurses, doctors, and chaplains to struggle with compassion fatigue. It's mainly trauma-specific, meaning that it's often caused by listening to traumatic stories time and time again. The constant bombardment to their minds and emotions as they listen to these stories, even watching them on the news, wears down their capacity to care any longer. It's not something people have terminally. It can be dealt with by rest, better boundaries, excellent self-care habits, and seeing a therapist always helps.

Burnout isn't trauma-specific. It's the most obvious reaction to long-term stress and, sadly, is very common! Burnout is emotional, mental, and physical exhaustion that occurs when several events in succession, or a combination of events, cause a high degree of stress on someone. Burnout could happen to the healthiest of people—yes, even *you*, but the early signs are often unrecognized and therefore ignored. Similar to compassion fatigue, recovering from burnout isn't difficult when the right self-care practices are put into place, such as healthy boundaries and rest. Encouraging people to be kind to themselves, to permit themselves to acknowledge that they're tired, causing a depleted capacity to cope anymore, is vital if they're to change the way they do things and get better.

YOU'RE A LIFE-LINE

I want to leave you with a few more valuable tools that I've used with every person or group of people I've been privileged to love, support, and counsel back to emotional health. Please know that when I say that, I'm rarely the only resource helping them. I'm not a hero that does this on my own because, as you'll remember, I advise you never to be their only "go to" person for help. It's too exhausting. I always try to work as part of a team with their doctors, therapists, spiritual support groups, and any other resource they're using to help them rise again. The tools I use that I'm sharing with you now will give you some strategic tactics to aid you in supporting them.

The main reason why it's so important to understand your value in the area of helping others in distress is that there are many times when they'll literally need a life-line, and you're it! You can bring hope, encouragement, and confidence to them. Even though you may not think you can do much, the impact you'll have is highly valuable. I want you to remember that fact when you offer your care and support to someone. Don't discount your worth or the magnitude of the impact you can have in their lives.

But what are the main goals of your care? There are several. It's important to help them reestablish a normal routine if possible. One of the most helpful steps is for them to have a sense of normalcy in as many areas of their lives as they can. It helps them feel empowered, which builds their confidence that there are things they can do to move forward and adjust where they need to manage the impact of the event that just crashed into their lives. This ties into their ability to regain a sense of control over areas of their lives that they may have lost or believed they'd lost.

ESTABLISHING A SENSE OF NORMALCY HELPS TRAUMA SURVIVORS FEEL EMPOWERED.

When we believe we've lost control, we can feel helpless. Feeling helpless can be crushing and can even tie into the guilt and shame we've talked about previously. This is especially true if people feel guilty or ashamed that they didn't do something to prevent the event

179

from happening or aren't doing something different to manage the consequences of the event. By enabling and empowering them to regain control, they grow in confidence to make appropriate and necessary decisions about their next steps, recovery, and future. The ultimate goal is to help them believe that they are valuable and important, that there are things they can do to mitigate the impacts of the event that caused the stress or trauma, and that they have it within themselves to reestablish their life and rise again. I'm not saying this will happen quickly. Everyone will obviously find their own rhythm and time frame along the way, but with your help, guidance, and support, it will happen quicker than it would without it.

PRACTICAL GUIDE FOR OFFERING HELP AFTER TRAUMA

You may have heard of the term psychological first aid. Just as physical first aid brings emergency medical attention to someone who's been physically injured, psychological first aid brings emergency care to a person in emotional trauma. It's a proven fact that the sooner you can reach them to offer emotional support, the more likely it is that they'll make a full recovery and could even recover faster.

Here are some proven step-by-step guidelines that I use when helping others in varying degrees of emotional stress, using the acronym **BRAVER**. By using these tips, you can help someone who's experiencing the most traumatic day of their life to feel brave enough to put one foot in front of the other to face their next minute, hour, day, or month.

- **B**e present, **B**e kind, **B**e patient, **B**e attentive
- **R**ecognize the symptoms and needs

- **A**sk and **A**cknowledge
- **V**alidate their responses and needs
- **E**ncourage and **E**mpower.
- **R**ecovery or **R**eferral.

BE PRESENT, BE KIND, BE PATIENT, BE ATTENTIVE

We already know the importance of actually being mentally, emotionally, and physically present with someone in distress. By being there, even without saying anything, you bring comfort. But how do you enter into their pain in the first place? First, pay attention by surveying the surrounding area for any potential danger signs if you're responding to a recent disaster or being in a potentially dangerous area. When safe to do so, approach them, move them to a safe place if necessary and offer your help. Allow them to choose whether they want it or not. Remember, it is always their choice, and at this moment, it's about them and their needs, nothing and no one else.

Always introduce yourself clearly first if you don't already know them especially if you're working with a disaster organization or non-profit, such as Red Cross, a Disaster Relief Team, or a Crisis Response Team. Be sure to explain who you're working with so that they know that you're there to help them. Remember that traumatized people can't usually take in a lot of information. They're in shock and may see your lips moving but cannot truly hear your questions or instructions, so speak clearly, slowly, and in short sentences. Be prepared to repeat yourself several times and be patient and kind to them. They need as much love and attention as you can give them. Connect with them by letting them know you're there to help. Watch their body language as well as listen carefully to the words they say. Be attentive so that they know you care. It helps to build trust.

RECOGNIZE THE SYMPTOMS AND NEEDS

Assess the person or people you're helping for any clues that will help you to meet their needs, such as if they need medical attention, or do they just need to borrow your phone to call a family member? Always meet immediate basic needs first, such as offering food and water if they're hungry or thirsty. Give them a blanket or coat if they're cold. These acts of kindness bring comfort and can decrease their stress levels. Look out for the signs and symptoms of trauma that we've gone over in this book and remember the five main areas where you're likely to see them, but don't be taken off guard by other things you may notice that I haven't mentioned. Remember, I didn't give you an exhaustive list of symptoms, and everyone responds differently, so look out for obvious symptoms caused by stress, but don't be alarmed if you don't see any. They may be noticeable later. Gain information by getting the facts about what happened to get a better idea of how to help them manage their symptoms. Let them know that you're there to help and that they're not alone. This is comforting and brings them some stability in that moment.

ASK AND ACKNOWLEDGE

Ask them to tell you their story so that you can continue to get more information about what happened, how it impacted them, and their subsequent needs. Do so by using open questions. Open questions are questions that don't have a yes or no answer to them, such as "Please tell me what happened?" rather than "Was there an earthquake?" Do you see the difference? In one example, you encourage them to say as much or as little as they want to, and with the other, they'll just say yes or no and then stop. Keep them talking to gain as much information as you can about what happened.

Ask them how they're doing, do they have any family nearby to help, what they need, or what they want help with. If they repeat themselves a lot, that's good because it's good for them; it's cathartic and helps them to destress. Always ask more questions if necessary to clarify what they tell you, without being nosy or too personal. It's important to make sure you've understood them correctly. If your questions aren't connected to their needs, don't pry into their personal lives by crossing boundaries. If they freely share, that's okay.

Acknowledge what they tell you. It helps to normalize things for them, which is calming. Acknowledge their reactions and their symptoms as well as the positive things that they did and try to encourage them if they're too focused on the negative things that didn't go well. Use your body language and good communication techniques to let them know you're listening and clearly hearing all that they're saying. It's very important to pay attention to them at all times while you're with them so that you hear and understand what they tell you. This helps you to continue to assess their needs. Listen more than you speak!

VALIDATE THEIR RESPONSES AND NEEDS

Validate them by explaining that their responses to the critical event are normal and that they're not going crazy. Some people feel embarrassed or afraid that they're losing their minds because they respond so strongly. Tell them that their stress responses are expected and are often seen in most people who have been through similar experiences. Explain the five main ways—physical, mental, emotional, spiritual, and behavioral—in which they could experience symptoms in response to the critical event. This helps them understand why they're responding the way they are and that it's common for people to react to a critical event. It helps them to allow themselves to "feel" what they're feeling and permits them to respond to how their bodies are responding without making them feel uncomfortable, embarrassed, or making them feel as if they have to pull themselves together. Too many people can feel embarrassed or ashamed about their responses, especially if they feel that others are worse off than they are, and therefore you shouldn't be helping them. Validate them by assuring them that their needs are just as important and that in that moment, you're there for them.

ENCOURAGE AND EMPOWER

Encourage them by telling them that they can rise again with the right help and support. That will naturally empower them to believe that they can pick themselves up, dust themselves off and face tomorrow. If there's been a major disaster, encourage them by telling them where to go for shelter, meals, and other resources nearby, such as feeding centers, distribution centers, or the FEMA tent. Help them feel empowered by encouraging them to come up with some ideas of things they can do in the first few hours or days to regain some normalcy in their lives and regain some control of their current situation. Suggestions, such as ensuring their diet is nutritious, exercising, volunteering at a shelter, or doing something positive for someone else in need, will help their recovery process. Empower them to make decisions for themselves. It restores their soul and helps them to believe that they can rebuild their lives.

RECOVERY OR REFERRAL

Give them facts and information about the recovery process and the timelines of recovery. Reassure them that with the right help and support, most people will recover well on their own in due course but that everyone recovers differently. Encourage them not to compare themselves or their speed of recovery to others. Share with them some appropriate self-care tips from the Defensive Strategies or Lines in the Sand chapters. Just by explaining these simple steps with people, you'll provide some very important support which will start them towards their own journey to healing.

As we discussed earlier, some people may need help that you're not qualified to give, so it's important to know what resources are available in your area so that you can refer them to the right kind of help at the right time; therapists, counselors, religious or faith leaders or social support groups. Let people know that if they're not seeing any improvement in their symptoms after a month to six weeks, they should see a trauma therapist or someone specializing in PTSD to make sure that they're receiving the correct type of help and support. You may not still be in their lives then, especially if you're on a deployment out of your own area. If in doubt, or if you see extreme symptoms that you know you're not qualified to deal with, always refer immediately.

It is very important to know that there are occasions when someone's symptoms are so acute that the individual could become "dysfunctional." I've only briefly mentioned dysfunction until now because unless you're a medical practitioner, therapist, or another suitably qualified person, you wouldn't be responsible for helping or caring for them professionally. However, I'd be providing a great disservice to you or anyone you help if I didn't remind you of some of

WHAT TO DO WHEN LIFE SUCKS

the dysfunctional symptoms here so that you know what to look for. These are just examples, most of them obvious, but it's important to be thinking along the lines that some people respond to trauma so strongly that not even you or I can help.

People may need immediate referral to the ER, a therapist, or other appropriate care levels, based on their needs. For example, chest pains, chronic shortness of breath, or other life-threatening symptoms. Other examples are finding someone in a catatonic state, having severe hallucinations or flashbacks, which could cause them to act out dangerously. These are severe symptoms and need to be treated as emergencies. In those circumstances, always refer immediately. Whether you help them personally or refer them immediately, you've still made a huge impact in their lives, possibly saving their lives just by being present. Therefore, you're a vital link in their chain of care, helping them rise again. ***RESURGAM!***

POST-TRAUMATIC GROWTH—THE RESURGAM FOREST

In the introduction, I wrote about a forest. You and I are that forest. A forest of tall, strong trees that have already, and will continue, to rise again and again from the pit of despair and the effects of acute stress or trauma. We can usually recover from injuries that cut us deeply due to just being alive and being human, but they don't need to bring death and destruction to our bodies and souls. I don't mean literal physical death; I mean death in the sense of being smothered and not thriving. I'm also referring to mental death, emotional death, spiritual death, behavioral death due to being suffocated by the cares of this world.

God is faithful to bring guidance, protection, and answers needed to strengthen, encourage and enable us to walk through the valleys of life, emerging on the other side different, in a good way, changed for the better. Am I saying that bad things won't still happen to us all? Obviously not. Living on this planet exposes us to tragic things. What I am saying is that we can and will survive the negative aspects of those bad things and grow despite them. Added to the many suggestions I've made in this book, you can do one more thing to ensure your survival and ability to have your own Resurgam moments, which is the most important thing of all. Believe in and trust God! If you already believe in God, trust Him, and put your confidence in Him. Know that He really does care for you and is more than capable of carrying you through all of the traumatic things you walk through in life. His promise is that you'll not only survive, but you'll thrive. How do I know? Look at this verse in Jeremiah 17:7-8, and I'll share what I think it's saying to us.

Most blessed is the man who believes in, trusts in, *and* relies on the Lord, and whose hope *and* confidence the Lord is. For he shall be like a tree planted by the waters that spreads **out its roots by the river; and it shall not see *and*** fear when heat comes; but its leaf shall be green. It shall not be anxious *and* full of care in the year of drought, nor shall it cease yielding fruit.

I translate this verse as you and I are the tree mentioned in it individually. We're each like a tree planted by the waters with roots that spread by the river. To me, that means that as long as we truly trust God in all ways and we keep our roots planted in Him (by staying connected to Him in prayer, worship, and by reading His Word), we'll never shrivel up and die, metaphorically, as a result of distressing things and challenges in life. The refreshing water in the river refers to attributes of God's character, namely as our provider, protector, our shield from danger, and our strength in battle, to name a few.

As long as our roots are planted by the river so that we're always being watered, we'll be fed and refreshed, sustained, and protected from the adverse effects of extreme heat, which are the difficult and painful seasons in life. When the heated battles come, this verse says we won't be afraid. The subject of fear is repeated twice in this short verse. Why? Because it's a very important part of what this passage is telling us. It's telling us that if we truly trust in God and in His ability to protect and guide us, we won't be afraid of the heat—the critical event, or of the outcome, the after-effects. In the first example, it says that instead of being afraid, our leaves will be green. Meaning we'll live. Yes, the heat of the battle may burn us and will even prune some parts of us that needed to be removed anyway, but it won't kill us, and our lives will remain green. That's a big deal.

The next time fear is refered to, the phrase "anxious and full of care" is used when referring to the year of drought that comes after the heat, which is the recovery period after the traumatic event happens. To me, the word drought reflects the emptiness, the dryness and lack of joy and peace that we often feel after a severe disruption to our normal lives. It encourages us by saying that we won't be anxious or full of care in the drought or during the recovery period. The cares of the world and the cares of life that pull us down won't worry us. The only way we can walk without fear or cares is to trust that God is going before us, sorting out all that needs to be sorted in order for us to survive and thrive. But then He encourages us again by saying that not only won't we be afraid in that season of drought, but we'll also bear fruit!

Having green leaves when extreme heat comes and growing fruit in a drought are powerful promises. They're both clearly telling us that heat will come, bad things will happen, but don't let fear crush you because you will get through it. It won't be easy or comfortable, but God will sustain you. The proof will be that you'll keep your lush green leaves during the heat, and better still, you will not stop yielding or bearing fruit. The fruit comes during the drought. Isn't that interesting. It comes after the battle is over. Our fruit is evidence, not only of our thriving but also of our future rising again. Our offspring, if you like, are our seeds that are planted as we pay it forward. It's all part of our post-traumatic growth, my friends, the growth that comes as a result of the fight.

GROWTH THAT COMES AFTER THE FIGHT

Post-traumatic growth creates a forest of strong trees that have stood the test of time and survived, sometimes against all odds. I wouldn't be leaving you feeling as confident as I possibly could at this point in the book if I didn't talk about the joys and miracles of post-traumatic growth. You can heal, you can have a good life again after a trauma that sucked the life out of you. You can rise again, and you can help others experience those same results. Post-traumatic growth, just as it sounds, refers to the fruit you bear, the positive changes that can take place in our lives both during and after traumatic experiences. Those excruciating seasons aren't all bad; they can, in fact, be good for us because we always learn incredibly valuable life lessons from them. Are they nice seasons to go through? Absolutely not. They're horrid most of the time. Yet each time I've gone through a tough season, I can see the benefits once I'm on the other side of it. So much so that I can confidently say that the lessons I've learned,

POST-TRAUMATIC GROWTH IS THE FRUIT YOU BEAR AND THE POSITIVE CHANGES THAT CAN TAKE PLACE IN YOUR LIFE DURING AND AFTER TRAUMATIC EXPERIENCES.

and the positive ways in which I've grown, are a direct result of that trauma are worth it. Would I want to do it all over again? No. But I'm grateful for the results, even though I'm still grieving the losses and always on a journey of recovery from the pain and cruelty that life can bring. Am I crazy to say that? Possibly, but let me explain.

We all usually come through painful, tragic, and very difficult times, wiser and stronger than we were before they crashed into our lives. They can help us mature in any, or all, of the five main areas we've spoken about throughout this book. They teach us how to manage our natural responses and symptoms when we're next faced with a critical situation. Highly disturbing situations can help us rearrange our priorities in life, reassess our boundaries and goals, and clarify our vision and purpose. Those are just a few examples of the positive aspects of recovery from uncomfortable and painful times that I've personally experienced, but I'm sure you could add to that list. Personally, I notice that each time I emerge from beneath the dark heavy cloud that weighs me down when I'm battling something painful, I always find that I have changed for the better in some way. I'm not always saying that I notice it immediately, but at some point, along the journey to wholeness, I can definitely see a difference. And you know what? The biggest difference I noticed was when I'd battled cancer and won the fight!

Do you remember at the beginning of that awful journey when God asked me if I was willing to lay down my life? I obviously thought he meant that I'd literally die, physically. But it wasn't until after I'd gone through that season that I noticed that I'd certainly died in many ways. Certain aspects of my old self, my old personality, character, and beliefs had changed. I'd been harshly pruned, like a fruit tree. It was painful but necessary. Without pruning the dead, useless branches that suck up the water and take up space that the "right" branches need, trees don't grow strong and healthy and don't produce good fruit. People are the same. We need the useless and unhealthy aspects of our lives pruned out to make room for the useful, healthy things to flourish.

Throughout my journey with cancer, I had no control over the outcome. I had no way to manipulate any aspect of it to ensure I'd get better. All I could do was go through the treatments and trust. I had to trust in God completely because I didn't trust that the chemo would work. It didn't help Mum, nor had it worked for several of my friends who'd lost their battles to the disease. Yes, I believed it could help fight cancer in some cases, but I didn't know for sure that that would be my story or that I'd survive the journey. With that scary revelation in my heart, in a moment of desperate surrender to the only person I could fully trust, I gave up all control in every area of my life. In that same moment when I sensed God testing me, I surrendered my plans, my dreams, my family, and my life. I was willing to die. I'm not saying I gave up hope. I still had plenty of that. I'm saying that I gave up control and trusted the journey. In trusting God and His plans and purposes for me, I learned the most powerful and valuable lesson about complete trust and total reliance on Him. I was that tree in the verse I just shared, and the more I surrendered to Him, the more He gave me the faith to not be afraid.

When I go through hard times now, does it always mean I get the outcome I want? No. Do I get my way? No. But it does mean that I have peace and freedom to fully allow Him to show me the way, to guide me through those painful times, and to teach me what I need to learn in the school of hard knocks. Everything I've ever gone through, whether good or bad, has taught me so many valuable lessons. I've noticed so many amazingly wonderful changes in my maturity, emotional strength, spiritual strength, fortitude, compassion for others in pain, deeper love and appreciation for my family and friends, healthier boundaries, and a much better sense of humor! I'm a better wife, Mum, Granny, friend, chaplain, public speaker, instructor, daughter, and sister because of the painfully positive lessons I've learned, and that's all proof of post-traumatic growth. All great fruit.

TRANSFORMATION

Post-traumatic growth transforms us, like a caterpillar going into a chrysalis and coming out as a butterfly. Just as we all die a form of death of our old selves, our old "normal" lives, to make room for the new version of ourselves and our new lives, caterpillars do the same thing. They die, in a strange way, so that they can be transformed into beautiful butterflies. When they're in their chrysalises, certain hormones in their bodies digest their flesh over a few days, until nothing is left but a liquid inside the chrysalis, like caterpillar soup, together with some highly organized groups of cells which will then form into the butterfly's body parts. Once the caterpillar's body is fully digested, the highly organized cells use the soupy liquid to form the wings, legs, eyes, antennae, and other parts of the butterfly's new body. Imagine dying and digesting yourself in order to grow into a better you. It sounds awful, doesn't it? And yet, we all go through a similar death mentally, emotionally, physically, behaviorally, and spiritually as we transform into our post-traumatic growth selves. Tragic things crush us, bruise us and kill certain parts of us, but it's not all bad. Some aspects of who we are need to die for the new growth to be released without being hindered or overshadowed. It's part of the pruning process, but our stories don't end there.

I'm sure you'll agree that a butterfly is usually far more beautiful and graceful than a caterpillar. It has a more exciting life in my opinion too. Imagine the difference between crawling on the ground as an ugly grub compared to being able to wow us with its beautifully painted wings and graceful flight. Post-traumatic growth can make you a more beautiful person and give you wings so that you can fly!

We've talked about what post-traumatic growth is, and I've given examples of it, but here are some personal stories from a couple of people that I've helped to demonstrate the liberating and strengthening power of it. I'll start with my own story of how grief first felt to me. My journeys through grief have taught me much. Now when I grieve, I'm not scared of my powerful responses; I'm far more comfortable with the process. I understand exactly what my grief responses are and can recover much easier than I used to.

∾🙰🙰∾

Grief! The pain of loss, the shock, and trauma that feels all too familiar. I've been there so many times before for various reasons, and each time I feel numb, I shut down mentally and emotionally as I try to find my feet and acclimate to my "new normal" world, yet again! Grief makes me feel as if I'm being tossed about by a huge wave that crashes over me, trying to hold me down, sucking the life out of me by drowning me as it smashes me into the rocks, then pressing me to the sandy bottom of the ocean with such a heavy weight that I have no strength to push back. It drags me along with the tide, grating my skin along the rough surface of the sand and smaller crushed rocks beneath me. The pain of grief is like salty seawater that stings my new open wounds. Momentarily as the strong current rolls me 'round and up, I'm suddenly being pushed out into fresh air, and in my panic to survive, I gasp for a breath while I have time—just one, but my timing is off. As I'm sucking the fresh air into my lungs, I don't see the next wave; I inhale saltwater. It tastes foul. I choke and gag. It stings my eyes so much that I can't open them to see where I am or to get my bearings. I question how to get out of the water? I can't see clearly enough to know the way out! Every toss and tumble of another wave crashing over me brings more injuries, more pain, more fear, worse vision, and a greater lack of clear direction. My brain feels numb, and my ability to think clearly fades. My energy is depleted, and I feel lifeless.

Suddenly, miraculously, the strong wave subsides, allowing my body to right itself. I can feel the sand beneath my feet, so I quickly press against it as I push myself up to a standing position. It's only then that I can breathe again properly, and I suck in as much air as I can to fill my oxygen-starved lungs. As I open my eyes, I notice that the water seems calmer. I can finally see which direction to drag myself to so that I can escape my watery grave, the depth of despair that comes with the pain of loss. I then notice that the water is only hip-deep, and once I'm up, I'm not drowning at all. I try to wade out of the water to safety, but, as I said, grief comes in waves, so just before I get to a safe place, another big wave comes at me from behind, without warning, and knocks me down again. The current sucks me back out to sea again. This time I'm more prepared, less frightened because I know what to do. I got through this once, so I'm more confident and tell myself that I'll get through this wave again. This time I'm able to swim through it, and as I break through to the surface of the water, I'm cresting the wave, allowing it to carry me to shore!

Grief is now like an old acquaintance. I understand its process, and when it knocks me off my feet with more emotional pain, I've learned just to do what I can to keep afloat, keep breathing, keep my body safe by relaxing, resting, and refueling it with healthy eating and plenty of fluids and fresh air. Then when I'm able to stand to my feet, lift my head out of the murky water, I can clearly see again and know where to go and how to get there to complete this journey. I feel safe again. I know how to handle the waves now. I can anticipate and trust the process rather than fighting it or "stuffing" the emotions and feelings down, or going into denial. I know that everything I go through when I'm grieving is normal, and I understand that it is ok not to be ok. I can and will rise again. Resurgam.

ৡ ঙ৩ঙ৩ঙ৩ ৡ

My life was completely broken and in pieces. It's been a little over a year since I was in the epicenter of trauma, and when I look back, I realize just how much better off I am now. Trauma, when handled and triaged correctly, can have an amazingly positive impact on someone's life. My life was coasting. I wasn't living for the Lord, and the enemy had me exactly where he wanted me, completely out of gear and in neutral. Trauma, although not the nicest thing in the world, was the thing that kick-started my life and put me back in gear. I began pressing in and spending time with the Lord, reading my bible, and creating a positive community via my church. Relationships in my family were re-established and became stronger; truths and struggles were shared throughout my family, bringing healing to everyone. I truly believe the breakthroughs would never have happened without trauma and the Lord. The Lord showed me not only how good He is but also how I can trust him with everything. I can look back on this experience and use the situations in it to stand on when my faith is tested today. Nowadays, I am far more aware of how trauma can happen and how to handle it. I understand how people feel when in trauma and know what to expect if it were to ever happen again in mine, or my family's life.

⊰ ୯୨ ୯୨ ୯୨ ⊰

After experiencing initial layers of loss, I didn't know which way was up; I soon understood why I was reacting and responding to the trauma I had experienced the way I was. As I healed, I learned how to give words to the emotions and feelings I didn't know how to express or deal with before. I truly believe because of Fran's help; I was saved from years of cycling through the same destructive patterns because of the wounding I had experienced in trauma. A year after the initial trauma, I was more aware of triggers and emotions that could rise up, and I had the right tools to deal with them. Now, after the fact, I have become a better version of myself. The 2.0 version. Healed, put back together in a stronger and transformed way. I come at conversations with others from a different perspective and understand how to love them and myself better.

⊰ ୯୨ ୯୨ ୯୨ ⊰

The privilege of helping others in trauma isn't without risk and sacrifice. It's exhausting and can be traumatizing work, so please keep yourself healthy. The more tragic and traumatic the calls that I respond to are, and the more frequently I'm called out to help others, the more I've had to find things to do that bring me joy, rest, and fun, to restore my soul. I've got to be far more careful to balance the effects of my work with soul-restoring, refueling self-care activities.

RISING AGAIN—LITERALLY

One time when I noticed that my usual self-care activities weren't helping me to rest properly and weren't restoring my soul as much as they did before, I was deployed to the Montecito Mudslides in Santa Barbara in January 2018. I was the team lead, overseeing Chaplains from Foursquare Disaster Relief Ministries. We provided emotional and spiritual care to the community and I was there for three weeks. While I was there, I met a wonderful Danish man called Keld, a Santa Barbara police officer. Keld is a man of incredible compassion for people, which he demonstrates daily in a variety of ways. One of his many talents is that of a baker. He bakes the most delightful sourdough loaves of bread, Danish pastries, pizzas, and other treats. When he's not selling his bread at functions and pop-up sales, he gives it away to his friends, colleagues, and anyone else he feels would appreciate the selfless gift of a wonderfully fresh sourdough loaf or baked treat.

Keld and I have in common a deep passion for people in need, especially needs resulting from trauma. Whereas I respond to disasters to provide emotional and spiritual care by listening to people and helping them plug into resources for continued care and recovery, Keld bakes sourdough bread and breaks it with those he finds along the way. It's a very reverential experience for him and for them. He takes all of his supplies with him, traveling into disaster-torn countries, finds a local group of people who've lost just about everything, and with incredible simplicity, he teaches them how to make bread for themselves. He's noticed that people come alive when they experience this. It brings them hope; it empowers them with confidence that they, like the bread they make, can rise up and find something life-giving that strengthens them. They experience joy in the midst of their pain and hope in their recovery. It enables them to be creative as they explore the art of baking. It allows them to give to others as they share their loaves with friends and neighbors. It helps them to provide support to others who're unable to find wholesome bread or food. These are all wonderful examples of their post-traumatic growth, aided by a man who's love for people brings positive change, creating a positive impact, not only on them but also on their community. They're rising again and paying it forward.

As Keld and I have come to know each other, he's patiently taught me the amazing art of baking sourdough breads. We've become great friends, enjoying a mutual journey of baking, and helping others in crisis. But little did I know just how much he would impact my life. What Keld taught me has opened up the most amazing journey of personal healing that I could have ever imagined. I'm experiencing the same empowerment and joy that he's brought to others in Santa Barbara and on his deployments. Baking bread each week has become my sanity saver, my self-care hobby, my mind calmer, and my soul restorer. Creating wholesome, delicious breads in my own kitchen fills me with such joy, I can't explain it. He and I laugh together about how addicting it is to both of us. It's changed my life in ways I didn't expect.

BAKING ARTISAN BREAD IN MY OWN KITCHEN HAS CHANGED MY LIFE IN WAYS I DID NOT EXPECT.

As I see the smiles on people's faces when I give them a warm, fresh homemade loaf, I understand more about the impact it has on them. Just as much as I enjoy baking it, they enjoy receiving it. Baking bread has become a lifeline to me. I get lost in the world of artisan whole grains that I now buy and mill myself. My soul comes alive when my hands feel the sensation of the soft flour mixing with the water as I squeeze the ingredients through my fingers, experiencing the touch and feel of simple ingredients that create a life-giving morsel to appreciative mouths. As I go through the process of caring for the starter, mixing the ingredients, kneading, resting, fermenting, shaping, proving, and baking, I see so many similarities between the process of baking a loaf of bread to the process of healing from trauma. But that's for another book! Suffice to say; this new hobby has done more for my mental health, more to restore my joy, and more to increase my capacity to rise again—like a loaf does—and continue to care for others than I could have imagined. This is another example of the post-traumatic growth transformation I've gone through.

A NEW OPPORTUNITY FOR GROWTH

This week, as I came to the end of writing this book, I received some difficult news. I was diagnosed with a heart condition that I have no idea what the prognosis is at the time I write this. The doctor said I'm in heart failure. That sounds so dramatic, as if I'm dying as I type this, but all it means is that my heart isn't working as it should. I don't like the word failure. I won't fail! My heart won't fail! Once again, my life is in God's hands, and yes, I'm willing to lay it down again. Why? Because I trust Him. Jesus rose again after death, so I can, too—metaphorically speaking. His old life died at Calvary, and He had a

Resurgam moment. When He rose again to his new life, He came back stronger, more powerful, and He's faithful to show me how to get through this so that my old life can be replaced with new life too.

I've learned from experience that Jesus is trustworthy, faithful, and good, so I'm not as scared this time as I was with cancer. I'm a tree that has stood the test of time, and I'm more firmly planted than I was before. My roots go deeper into the river than they did before, and I will continue to have green leaves and bear good fruit. Am I angry about it? Yes. Am I frustrated about it? Yes, of course, because it will change the course of my plans for this year, and maybe for life, but I will adapt and overcome as I always do. But am I scared? Nope.

I feel at peace, strong, safe in God's hands, and I trust Him completely. Before cancer, I'd have reacted in fear, but this time I'm calm. I've been through so many very difficult times in my life, way too many to write about in this book. But I can tell you now that my response to this new diagnosis is more proof to myself that I've grown in my faith, in my resolve to survive, in my ability not to panic, and in my belief that God's got my back. That's post-traumatic growth.

I'm confident that no matter what, just like the trees in our forest, I'll grow in strength, wisdom, and courage through this next ordeal, and along the way, I'll learn more about myself. I'll probably learn even more about the heart's various conditions, mentally, emotionally, physically, behaviorally, and spiritually than I now know, which will teach me more about how to help others' hearts heal. So, remember, nothing is wasted! Just like the new trees that are rising again in our wonderful forest, and like the wonderful fresh loaf of organic sourdough bread that I'm baking in the oven right now, I too shall rise again. *RESURGAM!*

I SHALL RISE AGAIN

MEET FRAN GRAHAM

Fran Graham serves as the Deputy Director for the Office of Emergency Management for her county in Montana. With an extensive background in law enforcement, the medical field, Search and Rescue, Community Emergency Response Training, International Foursquare Disaster Relief, Fire and Police Chaplaincy, and Critical Incident Stress Management, she provides a wealth of knowledge and expertise to those in crisis and psychological trauma. As well as responding to local emergencies and large-scale disasters, Fran is an ordained Foursquare Pastor and a Chaplain offering pastoral care. Fran works with individuals and groups who've experienced traumatic events and need uniquely adapted support systems and interventions.

Fran is passionate about holistic health, including "self-care" and healthy boundaries. She encourages others to establish these vital principles in their lives as part of their daily routine. She teaches them about the importance of recognizing signs and symptoms of grief, critical stress, burnout, compassion fatigue, and trauma and what to do about them. As an accredited instructor on topics such as Critical Incident Stress Management, National and International Disaster Response, Chaplaincy and Psychological Trauma, Fran trains emergency responders and civilians who are interested in gaining the necessary skills which equip them to offer peer support and crisis intervention to members of their community both nationally and internationally.

Fran is a wife, a mother, and a grandmother. She has been married to her soul mate and best friend, Rob, for over 38 years. They have lived both overseas and in the US. They have four grown sons, three daughters-in-law, and her wonderful grandchildren are the lights of her life and great for her self-care needs!

When Fran is not responding to tragic situations or mentoring others, she replenishes her resources by finding rest and peace outside in nature. She loves outdoor adventures such as hiking (especially through forests), camping, traveling, and horseback riding. When she is home, she hosts fun parties, has friends over for dinner, plays silly games, and relaxes with her family.

To learn more or to invite Fran to speak at your event:

WWW.FRANHGRAHAM.COM